MANCHESTER
PAST & PRESENT

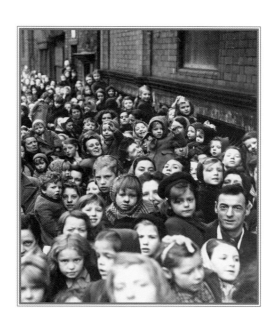

A Lancashire lass in shawl and clogs selling a newspaper to a workman as he passes through Albert Square, 1930s.

Manchester
Past & Present

Chris E. Makepeace

SUTTON PUBLISHING

First published in the United Kingdom in 2001 by
Sutton Publishing Limited exclusively for
WHSmith, Greenbridge Road, Swindon SN3 3LD

Paperback edition first published in 2004

British Library Cataloguing in Publication Data
A catalogue record for this book is available from the British Library.

ISBN 0-7509-3880-3

Illustrations

Front endpaper: Central station between the wars.
Back endpaper: G-Mex Centre, formerly Central station. (*D. Brearley*)
Half title page: The scene outside Wood Street Mission, possibly during the 1930s, as children queue up waiting to enter the building. The reason for such a crowd is not clear, but a look at their clothing suggests it may be winter and that the event may be a Christmas party.
Title page: Passengers leaving a train that has just arrived at Victoria station, early 1950s. It is not known where the train had come from, but east or central Lancashire are likely. Those getting off the train are probably on their way to work in the offices, warehouses and other business premises in central Manchester.

Typeset in 11/14pt Photina and produced by
Sutton Publishing Limited, Phoenix Mill,
Thrupp, Stroud, Gloucestershire GL5 2BU.
Printed and bound in England by
J.H. Haynes & Co. Ltd, Sparkford.

Contents

The west end of Manchester Cathedral after the building had been cleaned in the mid-1960s. Note the position of the statue of Oliver Cromwell before it was moved from the junction of Cateaton Street and Victoria Street to Wythenshawe Park in 1968.

Introduction

In 2002 Manchester hosts the Commonwealth Games and many thousands of people will visit the city and surrounding areas. It is to be hoped that as well as attending sporting events, they will also take the opportunity to explore Manchester and discover something of the city's history and achievements. The stadium where many of the events are taking place is located in an area which has been called 'Eastlands' and which is, in effect, the old district of Bradford. The changes taking place in this part of Manchester are reflected in the changes which are taking place in other parts of the city, not least in the city centre. The face of Manchester is changing at a rate faster than at any other time in its history. Familiar buildings and landmarks are disappearing and new buildings springing up in their place. New vistas are being opened up as buildings are demolished, some of which may not have been seen for almost two centuries. In this book an attempt has been made to show some of the changes that have taken place in central Manchester over the last 150 years since the advent of photography. Unfortunately, space precludes the inclusion of the suburbs where there have also been many changes over the last 100 years or so.

The Commonwealth Games will bring many people from abroad to Manchester. Many of these visitors will know little of the history of the city and its achievements. They may have heard of Manchester and associate it with sport because they have heard of Manchester United, a football club that started in Newton Heath, but eventually moved to a ground outside the boundaries of the city from which it takes its name. However, the connection of the name 'Manchester' with a single event, organisation or product is not new. In the 19th century many shops and stores overseas had 'Manchester departments', which dealt in cotton goods, most of which originated in Lancashire. In 1847 the *People's Journal* said that Manchester was to be associated with the use of steam power on a large scale to drive its machinery. In the field of economics, Manchester was not only the centre from which the Anti-Corn Law League was organised in the 1830s and 1840s, but also gave its name to a school of economic thought, the Manchester School, which, put simply, wanted few government restrictions on imports and exports to encourage other countries to remove their restrictions which, it was believed, would stimulate the export of cotton and other manufactured products.

Although Manchester began to be an economic force in the country at the end of the 18th century and at the beginning of the 19th, reaching its peak in the late 19th century, it had already been an important town in the south-east Lancashire area from the Middle Ages and possibly earlier. The first settlement in the area was a small civilian *vicus* which developed around the Roman fort overlooking the confluence of the rivers Irwell and Medlock. It is worth noting that the Romans occupied Manchester for over 300 years, a period longer than that which has elapsed since Cross Street Chapel was established in 1694 and St Ann's Church built in 1712. Modern Manchester did not develop from this settlement, but from one which grew up during the so-called Dark Ages overlooking the confluence of the rivers Irwell and Irk, close to where Manchester Cathedral and Chetham's School are now located.

Although there is only the briefest of references to Manchester in Domesday Book, it is sufficient to indicate that it was the centre for an ecclesiastical parish and that there was an important landowner responsible for the area. During the Middle Ages Manchester developed as a market town with its own market and fair, and it appears to have been as important, if not more important, than Salford, which claimed jurisdiction over the area. Unlike some towns, it did not achieve borough status until 1838. There were those who argued in the 1830s that this helped the growth of Manchester as there were few restrictions on who could set up in business within its boundaries.

By the 16th century textiles played an important role in the local economy with woollen cloth being exported to the continent. Manchester was home to several very

The *Manchester Evening News* was founded in 1868 and has been an important component of Manchester's media industry ever since. In order to distribute it throughout the city centre, horses and two-wheeled carts were used to deliver copies of the latest edition to street newspaper sellers. This photograph of the 1930s, taken in Albert Square, shows the latest editions on their way to newsagents and street sellers in central Manchester.

wealthy cloth merchants. One of these was Humphrey Chetham, who was responsible in the 17th century for leaving money to found Chetham's School and Chetham's Library, Europe's oldest free public library. Throughout the 17th and early 18th centuries Manchester continued to grow in importance and influence in the south-east Lancashire area. Gradually the foundations of modern Manchester and its economic and commercial importance were laid.

By 1750, although Manchester was still a market town, it had a population of around 17,000 and was one of the largest towns in Lancashire. Half a century later, although technically still a market town, its population had swelled to over 70,000 and by 1851 the population of what is described today as 'central Manchester' had reached almost 187,000, after which it began to decline. More recently the population of the central area, after reaching a very low level after the Second World War, has started to increase as former warehouses and offices buildings have been converted into apartments and flats and new housing has been built on sites of buildings which have been demolished. Central Manchester is again an area where people are now living as well as working and enjoying themselves.

The growth of Manchester was further encouraged by the development of the canals, which enabled raw materials to be brought into the town and the finished products taken away relatively cheaply and efficiently. In the 19th century new forms of transport, namely the railway and later the Manchester Ship Canal, gave the city not only faster connections to other parts of the country and the ports, but also direct access to the sea.

Towards the end of the 18th century the adaptation of steam to drive machinery encouraged industry to establish itself in Manchester, taking advantage of cheap bulk transport and a plentiful supply of labour. Although the early users of steam power were the textile mills, it was not long before the engineering industry began to develop, manufacturing not only machines but also machine tools. During the 19th century engineering probably employed more people in Manchester than did those firms producing cotton yarn. Firms like Sharp Roberts, Beyer Peacocks and Whitworths became known all over the world for their products, many of which were exported not only to the Empire, but to other countries as well. By the middle of the 19th century Manchester was at the centre of a region that was said to contribute almost 40 per cent of the country's exports, a significant part of which was generated by the cotton industry. Fortunes were made (and lost) in the textile trade, as witness the amount of money left by people like John Owens and John Rylands.

Although Manchester did not produce much cotton yarn, it was the centre of the cotton textile trade with its many warehouses, the first of which was built in 1838 for Richard Cobden on Mosley Street. The arrival of the textile warehouses increased the pressure on those living in central Manchester, and those who could afford to moved away, into what are now the suburbs of Manchester. Gradually, in the late 19th and early 20th centuries, the suburbs were drawn into Manchester and incorporated within the city's boundaries. Many of the warehouses of the latter half of the 19th century still remain, especially in the George Street/Princess Street areas.

Although Manchester is regarded by some as an industrial city, it has to be remembered that it does have a cultural and educational side. The first public library to be established

Pedestrians walk across the Esplanade at Piccadilly on a warm summer's day, *c.* 1902. The tower in the background is on Lewis's store and the tall building on the right is the rebuilt Mosley Hotel.

under the 1850 Public Libraries Act was opened in Manchester. The city was at the forefront of the demands for free, rate-supported education for the whole country. It was in Manchester that one of the earliest higher education facilities was established which did not require those seeking to gain admission to be a member of the Church of England – Owens College, which celebrates its 150th anniversary in October 2001. It was in Manchester that Charles Hallé established the first professional symphony orchestra in the country in 1858, and Annie Horniman sought to establish a repertory theatre in 1908. These are just a few of the things that have taken place in Manchester over the years, discoveries and introductions which owe much to the attitude of individual Mancunians and to those running the administration of the town.

Since 1750 there have been many changes in Manchester. In the centre of the city only a few buildings from that period still remain, such as Chetham's School and St Ann's Church. Others buildings have survived, but they have been rebuilt or even relocated, such as Manchester Cathedral, Cross Street Chapel and the Wellington Inn. There are more buildings from the latter half of the 18th century, but development has seen these reduced to a mere handful on streets like Byrom Street, St John's Street, Lever Street, Princess Street and isolated cases on the fringe of the city centre. Many more buildings survive in central Manchester from the 19th century although 20th-century events and redevelopment has meant that many of these are concentrated in specific areas and not throughout the city. For example, there are still many warehouses to be found in the George Street area, along Princess Street and Whitworth Street.

Over the last 250 years there have been many changes in Manchester. Many people have been affected by these changes as industry and commerce have been forced to adapt to new circumstances. So it is with the buildings of the town. For a city to continue to be vibrant and grow, change is essential. Just as machines become obsolete, so also do buildings. It is possible to convert some to new uses, but there are those which have to be demolished. Sometimes changes are forced on the residents by outside events, but when these happen, it is necessary to look on the bright side and take the opportunity to

As the redevelopment of Piccadilly Gardens goes ahead, the Esplanade has been closed for refurbishment and to allow a new building to be erected on part of the site. This view looks towards Royal Buildings at the junction of Mosley Street and Market Street. Just beyond Royal Buildings is the former Lewis's store with the base of the tower visible as in the picture opposite. (*D. Brearley*)

Work to improve the Knott Mill area, 1909. The arched brickwork on the right formed part of the Deansgate Tunnel on the Rochdale Canal which was being opened up and reduced in length. As usual, where there are men working, there are spectators, several of whom can be seen watching proceedings from the fence in front of the Railway Hotel. (*Manchester Local Studies Unit*)

improve things. In the case of Manchester, large changes have tended to take place towards the end of the century. So it is today with the rebuilding of parts of the city centre after the IRA bomb in 1996. *Manchester Past & Present* provides an opportunity to look at some of the buildings and scenes of earlier decades and what is there today. Change may not be appreciated by everyone, but it is essential if the city is to remain an important influence in the corridors of power. There is room for both old and new in a city. Some areas change regularly, but in others change is a rarity. Often, the need for change is imposed by outside forces rather than generated internally. Whatever the cause, change is inevitable and Manchester has always moved with the times.

The Cathedral & its Environs

Although Deansgate is one of central Manchester's oldest streets and a busy east–west route across the city centre, little was done to improve its overall appearance and to widen it until the 1860s when the part between St Mary's Gate and Peter Street was widened. In the 1870s the part from the Cateaton Street/Victoria Street junction to St Mary's Gate was improved when the remaining part of Smithy Door was demolished and replaced by Victoria Buildings. The new building cost £140,000 and included shops, offices, a hotel and Victoria Arcade. This postcard shows the junction of Deansgate and St Mary's Gate, with Victoria Buildings in the centre of the picture. During the Manchester blitz of Christmas 1940, Victoria Buildings were so severely damaged that the ruins had to be demolished shortly afterwards.

Smithy Door lay adjacent to the Market Place and had been used as an overflow market area in the late 18th century. The area was one of the oldest parts of central Manchester, and scavengers were appointed by the Court Leet to keep it clean. During the 1830s part of Smithy Door was cleared and separated from the Market Place when Victoria Street was constructed to provide an improved link between Market Street and the recently completed Bury New Road over Hunt's Bank Bridge. This photograph was taken around 1864 and shows the remaining buildings that were demolished a decade later when Victoria Buildings were erected.

When Victoria Buildings were erected, the corner overlooking the junction of Cateaton Street, Victoria Street and Deansgate was designated for use as a hotel. The Victoria Hotel was reported to have 140 rooms, together with restaurants and a billiard room with sixteen tables. This view was taken from in front of the cathedral in the early 20th century. At that time a single room cost 2s 6d and a double room 6s 6d a day. Guests paid an additional 1s for a fire in their bedroom and the same amount if they wanted a cold bath in the bathroom! The cost of breakfast ranged from 1s 6d to 2s 6d while the *table d'hôte* dinner started at 5s. The hotel was destroyed when Victoria Buildings were hit during the Manchester blitz.

After the Second World War the process of rebuilding the heart of Manchester took a long time to get under way. As a temporary measure some of the sites of the bomb-damaged buildings that had been demolished were turned into car parks while others were landscaped. This postcard shows the site of the former Victoria Buildings around 1960 after it had been landscaped. On the left are the former Grosvenor and Deansgate Hotels, which were demolished in the late 1960s. The buildings on the right, fronting on to Victoria Street, were demolished around the same time. In the mid-1960s the white building was occupied by the Measham Motor Sales Organisation and next door Central Chambers provided accommodation for a beautician, a furrier, a firm of vermin destroyers and a firm of consulting engineers.

During the late 1960s and early '70s the area around Manchester's Market Place, known as the Shambles, was transformed as part of a massive redevelopment stretching from High Street to the River Irwell. The only buildings which remained from the pre-war period were the Wellington Inn and Sinclair's Oyster Bar, which were raised 5 feet on a concrete plinth to fit in with the new building levels. In June 1996, after the area had been devastated by an IRA car bomb, further major redevelopment took place when all the buildings in an area bounded by Corporation Street, Cateaton Street, Deansgate and St Mary's Gate were demolished. One of the last sites to be developed was that where Victoria Buildings once stood, shown here in the summer of 2001. (*D. Brearley*)

In the Middle Ages the market place was an important focal point in many communities and was often close to the parish church. Manchester Market Place, which lay a short distance from the parish church, was relatively small compared with that in some other towns. When the town began to grow and attract more people to its market, it became very congested so that by the end of the 18th century there were several different places where markets were held. In 1821 the Lord of the Manor, who collected the market tolls, decided to centralise all the markets at Smithfield although a few stalls were allowed to remain in the Market Place itself as this photograph of about 1858 shows. The building with the large optician's sign (a pair of glasses) is the Wellington Inn (see page 22).

As well as the market stalls, there were also numerous shops in the Market Place together with several inns and hotels. Throughout the latter half of the 19th century there was much congestion in the area when the stalls were erected so in 1891 the City Council decided to remove the remaining stalls, a move that met with approval from most people. This 1930s photograph shows the changes which had taken place since the mid-19th century, including the erection of the Cotton Waste Dealers and Coal Exchange on the site of the former Victoria Fish and Game Market.

During the Manchester blitz the Market Place was devastated with only the Wellington Inn and Sinclair's Oyster Bar escaping serious damage. The result was that many of the once-familiar buildings there were demolished. This is the scene the morning after the blitz, looking past the Wellington Inn towards Old Millgate and the cathedral, past where the Falstaff Hotel and the premises where Yates, a well-known flower and gardening shop, used to stand.

After the war the area surrounding the Market Place underwent a transformation. In the 1950s the site at the corner of Corporation Street and Market Street, backing on to the Market Place, was developed by Marks & Spencer while later developments in the 1960s and early '70s resulted in the area which had been Manchester's Market Place being completely built over. The IRA bomb of 1996 presented the opportunity for further redevelopment. This resulted in the Wellington Inn and Sinclair's Oyster Bar being relocated and a huge Marks & Spencer store erected on an enlarged site which incorporated not only the store's original site, but also that of the two pubs. (*D. Brearley*)

One of central Manchester's best-known groups of buildings is the Wellington Inn and Sinclair's Oyster Bar, known as the Old Shambles. The Wellington Inn, which became a public house in the early 19th century, was timber-framed and may have dated from the 16th century. When it became a public house, the upper floor was leased, at various times, to different tenants. In 1859 the tenant was Mr Bowen, optician and 'practical mathematical instrument maker', who started his business in 1802. By the time the top picture was taken, in the early 20th century, the upper floor was occupied by a shop selling fishing tackle. At the far end of the block stood Sinclair's, a brick building dating from the 18th or early 19th century, which became an oyster bar during the latter half of the 19th century. On the right is the Cotton Waste Dealers Exchange, the ground floor of which was used by fish and game merchants. This building was destroyed in the blitz. In the post-war redevelopment of the area, the Shambles were raised to fit in with the new development. The 1980s photograph (left), shows the two buildings after restoration.

When the Market Place area was replanned after the 1996 IRA bomb, the location of the Old Shambles was a problem because it prevented the large-scale redevelopment of the Marks & Spencer site. As a result, it was decided to take down both the Wellington and Sinclair's and move them about ¼ mile to a location close to the cathedral. At the same time Sinclair's was turned through 90° so that it ended up at right angles to the Wellington Inn, as seen here. (*D. Brearley*)

Two of Manchester's statues have also been relocated since the Second World War. In 1968 the statue of Oliver Cromwell (left) which stood at the junction of Cateaton Street, Deansgate and Victoria Street was moved to Wythenshawe Park. The Cromwell statue was given to Manchester in 1876 by Mrs Abel Heywood in memory of her first husband, Alderman Goadsby, who had presented the statue of Prince Albert in the Albert Memorial to the city after the Prince's death in 1861. The Abraham Lincoln statue (right), unveiled in 1919, was originally located in Platt Fields, but was moved to central Manchester when Lincoln Square was created in the 1990s. (*D. Brearley*)

The major redevelopment which has taken place in the Corporation Street/Market Place area since the IRA bomb of 1996 has resulted in many familiar buildings being restored and given new leases of life with new uses. This is the case with the former printing offices that dominated the corner of Corporation Street and Withy Grove. These offices were once the home of the *Sporting Chronicle* and *Manchester Evening Chronicle*. The latter was published for the first time in 1897 by Edward Hulton, who had also started the *Sporting Chronicle* and *Athletic News* in the 1880s. He continued to be involved with all three papers until 1923 when ill-health forced him to sell. The titles were acquired by Allied Newspapers, later Kemsley Newspapers, which were responsible for erecting the building seen here in the late 1920s. It was later claimed that the offices were the 'world's largest newspaper office'. Since that time the building has had a number of different names, all associated with the newspaper industry. However, changing methods of production and an increase in the size of lorries delivering newsprint meant that the building was not suitable for modern newspaper production so it was closed. It has now found a new lease of life as an entertainment complex known as 'the Printworks', which includes bookshops as well as cinemas. (*Modern photograph by D. Brearley*)

24

There has been a church on the site of the present Manchester Cathedral since before the Norman Conquest. This church was the parish church of Manchester and also served an area of about 60 square miles of south-east Lancashire, much of which now forms the City of Manchester. In 1421–2 Thomas de la Warre expressed concern about the provision made for the spiritual well-being of the inhabitants of the parish and obtained a charter to create a Collegiate Church where there were several priests to take services and visit the outlying areas. During the next hundred years the church was completely rebuilt and assumed the appearance shown here. Further changes took place in the 19th century when the building was 'restored'. In 1847 the Collegiate Church of St Mary, St Denys and St George became the centre of the new Manchester diocese and the former parish and Collegiate Church became Manchester Cathedral. To mark Queen Victoria's Diamond Jubilee in 1897, Manchester Cathedral added a new west porch in the area between the entrance from Victoria Street and the tower. When it was first completed, the porch presented a vivid contrast to the remainder of the building in that the stone appeared clean whereas the rest of the building was black from atmospheric pollution. This photograph should be compared with the one on page 10.

Cateaton Street is one of the oldest streets in central Manchester. Its name is derived from the Anglo-Saxon for 'hollow way', and it may have followed the course of the River Dene. In the Middle Ages it appears to have linked Old Salford Bridge to Old Millgate and the Market Place. In the 16th century it was said that the houses stood high above a sunken roadway, though there is no evidence of this today. Many of the buildings on Cateaton Street date from the mid- to late 19th century with Minshull House, close to the junction with Victoria Street, being the most interesting in both appearance and history. During the Manchester blitz of December 1940 many of the buildings fronting Cateaton Street were damaged and had to be demolished. This is Cateaton Street the morning after the blitz as firemen damp down the smouldering rubble.

After the war the Market Place side of Cateaton Street was redeveloped with tall office blocks while on the opposite side some of the original buildings remained. This photograph from the 1950s shows the view down Cateaton Street from Corporation Street with the new buildings on the left and the older buildings on the right. (*Manchester Transport Museum Society*)

The damage done to the 1950s buildings by the IRA bomb was so severe that they had to be demolished, which provided an opportunity to redesign the area. The result has been the closure of Cateaton Street to through traffic and the construction of a pedestrianised area linking Marks & Spencers with the former Corn Exchange (now known as The Triangle). (*D. Brearley*)

Running round one side of Manchester's manor house, now Chetham's College, was a street that gave access to the corn mills on the River Irk and eventually to Scotland Bridge, one of the crossing points of the river, and thence into the township of Cheetham. This road was Long Millgate, which still retains its old name and some of its original sharp bends. Between 1515 and 1930 the site on the right was occupied by Manchester Grammar School. The building shown here was erected in the 1860s to replace earlier buildings and enable the school to take more pupils. When Manchester Grammar School moved to Rusholme, the buildings were used for Long Millgate College, which trained mature students to become teachers. More recently they have been incorporated in Chetham's School of Music, which lies behind them in the buildings that formerly housed the clergy at the Collegiate Church. On the left-hand side of the road were a series of courts which, until the 1870s, contained timber-framed buildings from the 15th and 16th centuries. These were demolished and replaced by modern buildings in the 1870s and '80s.

A view of Poet's Corner on Long Millgate with the corner of the former Manchester Grammar School building in the background. The stone structure (centre) is the entrance to Chetham's School of Music, a gateway which, although it has been rebuilt in recent times, still retains the appearance it had when it was drawn by H.G. James around 1820. The new buildings on the right were constructed partly on the site of a building destroyed during the blitz and partly on the site of a building which once proclaimed itself to be the Old Swan Hotel. The corner of this building can just be seen on the top photograph on page 31. (*D. Brearley*)

The first Corn Exchange was opened in Manchester in 1837 in a building designed by Richard Lane. As the city grew in importance as a regional centre, so the old building became unsuitable and the decision was taken to build a new one. The site chosen was bounded by Hanging Ditch, Fennel Street and Cathedral Street and involved the complete demolition of an area of shops and warehouses. The new building, almost triangular in shape, consisted of an exchange floor, lit by the dome, and surrounded by a curtain wall containing offices. Work started on the new building in 1893 and each wing was opened as it was completed. The top photograph shows the Hanging Ditch façade of the building *c.* 1910 with porters and wagons of goods outside. During the 1970s and '80s the floor of the Exchange was used for stalls and events like postcard fairs. The building was severely damaged by the 1996 bomb and there were doubts whether it could be restored. Happily, it was, and, is now known as The Triangle, with restaurants and a number of boutique-type shops selling a range of goods from designer clothing to environment-friendly products. (*Modern photograph by D. Brearley*)

Victoria station was opened in 1844 by the Manchester & Leeds Railway (later the Lancashire & Yorkshire Railway) which shared it with the London & North Western Railway. On the left is the original station building, to which an additional floor had been added. As passenger traffic grew during the 19th century, the station was enlarged on several occasions. When this photograph was taken in 1878, Victoria station had about eight platforms and an impressive entrance, approached along Hunt's Bank from Victoria Street. In 1884 the LNWR moved to their own Exchange station, which was technically in Salford. Further expansion took place at the end of the 19th century so that by 1923 there were seventeen platforms at Victoria station.

During the last half of the 20th century the increased use of the private car has resulted in a sharp decline in the number of people travelling by train. This meant first the closure of Exchange station in 1969 and then the gradual transfer to Piccadilly station of most of the trains travelling between Liverpool, Yorkshire and the north-east of England and between Manchester and the Lancashire coast. Victoria station became under-used so it was decided to reduce the number of platforms and simplify the railway network around the station. Part of the station was developed, with an arena capable of holding over 15,000 spectators, and a multi-screen cinema, together with parking facilities. Now known as the 'Manchester Evening News Arena', it is used for sporting events as well as all types of musical shows. This photograph shows part of the new development and the arena from the bottom of Hunt's Bank.
(*D. Brearley*)

Linking Victoria station with Corporation Street is Todd Street, once known as Th'Owd Street and then Toad Street. This road originally stretched in an arc from Long Millgate to the Withy Grove/Fennel Street junction, but the creation of Corporation Street resulted in it being reduced in length. This is Todd Street in the 1960s, looking towards Victoria station. Until about 1829 the junction of Todd Street and Long Millgate was very narrow and referred to as 'Dangerous Corner', as it was difficult to see what was coming in the opposite direction. This danger was removed when the road was widened. The two-storeyed white building, partially hidden by City Buildings, was built about 1837 as the Collegiate Church's Jubilee Schools and may have been designed by Richard Lane. In the background is the entrance to Victoria station; the canopy indicates some of the destinations of the L&Y.

A modern view of Todd Street and Victoria station. Although the buildings on the right and the station itself have changed little over the years, the roof of the Manchester Evening News Arena behind the trees now replaces the train shed of the station while the buildings on the right of the upper picture are today a building site.
(D. Brearley)

Corporation Street was created in the middle of the 19th century to improve communications between central Manchester and the Cheetham Hill area and to reduce congestion in the Market Place and along Long Millgate. In 1846 the first section of Corporation Street was completed between Market Street and Fennel Street/Withy Grove and about four years later the new road was extended to Ducie Bridge, which solved some of the problems caused by congestion around the Market Place. Very quickly, Corporation Street was lined with tall buildings like these between Fennel Street and Todd Street. During the 1960s, when this photograph was taken, the two buildings on the left were occupied by a number of small businesses including representatives of cotton spinning firms, turf accountants, a photocopying consultancy and an employment agency.

In the 1970s the buildings between Fennel Street and Todd Street were demolished, as were those fronting on to Long Millgate. A Holiday Inn was to be built on the site, but there was little progress and Holiday Inns eventually became involved with the restoration and running of the Midland Hotel. For many years the site remained vacant, used as a car park, but with the growing demand for living accommodation in central Manchester it is now being developed partly as a residential area, shown here, with an information centre on the Long Millgate frontage. (*D. Brearley*)

Around the Royal Exchange

This spectacular photograph was taken during the Manchester blitz in December 1940 when the Royal Exchange was one of the buildings that were damaged. Astonishingly, it was possible to get part of the Exchange floor back into use within six weeks. The damaged area was boarded off until after the war.

In 1809 a new building, designed by Thomas Harrison, was opened at the bottom of Market Street; officially called the Commercial Building, it was known to most people as the Exchange. The building included a newsroom, bar and several small shops such as a tailor's and a hatter's as well as a dining room which could accommodate 300 diners. During the first half of the 19th century the Exchange was enlarged several times as its membership increased. This photograph was taken in the 1860s from the Market Place and shows part of the building and the royal coat of arms, granted by Queen Victoria after her first visit to the city, above the entrance.

In the mid-1860s the numbers using the Royal Exchange had increased to such an extent that the old building was too small. A larger building was erected, shown here c. 1905. The new Royal Exchange building was opened in two phases in 1871 and 1874. On days of 'High 'Change', a large number of businessmen descended on the Exchange and the surrounding area to discuss and transact business. The Exchange Street/Market Street corner of the building was dominated by a tower that was clearly visible along Market Street and Victoria Street while the Cross Street façade, shown here, was dominated by the large portico, removed when the Exchange was enlarged after the First World War. The floor of the Exchange, where many of the deals took place, was at first floor level while the ground floor was used for shops.

The demolition of the Cross Street portico changed the appearance of the Royal Exchange while the extension gave the building a more balanced appearance. During the interwar years membership of the Exchange gradually declined, but the building still provided the cotton industry with an important meeting place to transact business. After the Second World War the cotton industry continued to decline. In 1968 it was decided to close the Exchange floor, and the company that operated it moved into smaller offices, leaving the owners of the building with the problem of what to do with a large open area. This was eventually solved when the Royal Exchange Theatre was established on the floor of the Exchange itself, thus ensuring the future of the building. These two photographs show the Cross Street façade (top) and the Market Street frontage in 2001. (*D. Brearley*)

Compare these two pictures taken about 90 years apart and it will be seen that there have been relatively few changes in the appearance of the buildings. St Ann's Church, consecrated in 1712, has not changed in its overall appearance since the end of the 18th century. The changes that have taken place are in the use of the shops and the fact that traffic is now prohibited from entering the Square, thus creating a traffic-free area for shoppers and pedestrians. The greatest change to affect the buildings in St Ann's Square has been the extension of the Royal Exchange. When the photograph above was taken the shops included several shoe shops, a confectioner's, a bookseller's, a milliner's, a ladies' outfitter's and a silversmith's while the offices were occupied by a wide range of small firms, many of which were professional – solicitors, accountants and consulting engineers, for example. Today there is a similar range of shops and a café. (*Modern photograph by D. Brearley*)

In 1694 the followers of the Revd Henry Newcome completed a new place of worship on Cross Street. Newcome, a Presbyterian minister, had come to Manchester in 1656 to take up a position at the parish church and was ejected because he refused to accept the re-establishment of the Church of England as the only church in the country after the Restoration. The new chapel was built to replace a temporary one in what had been a barn off Shudehill. Newcome died in 1695, but the chapel continued to flourish. In 1715 it was severely damaged by rioters who supported the Old Pretender, but was restored with the help of £1,500 from the government. During the 18th century the chapel gradually changed from a Presbyterian Church to a Unitarian place of worship. During the latter half of that century, it began to attract many of the businessmen and merchants in Manchester as well as providing a place for the Manchester Literary and Philosophical Society to meet between 1781 and 1799. The chapel was described in 1929 as the 'best brick built building' in Manchester (top left), but it was destroyed in the Manchester blitz. After the war a new chapel was erected on the site (bottom left), a simple structure in keeping with the tenets of Unitarianism. In the late 1990s this building was replaced by a new chapel located on the ground floor of an office block (right). Thus, the presence of the Unitarian Church was preserved as well as continuing the use of the site for the second oldest place of worship in central Manchester. (*Modern photograph by D. Brearley*)

The road that is today known as Cross Street originally had several different names at intervals along its length. It was not until the 1820s or '30s that the road was given a single name. Originally, access from Cross Street to Market Street was through a narrow passage, but as part of the improvement of Market Street this was widened. The result was that vehicles were able to enter from Market Street and it became easier to reach the Town Hall on the corner of Cross Street and King Street. During the last 200 years the buildings on Cross Street have undergone many changes. This illustration dates from around 1910 when the Eagle Insurance Buildings (extreme left) had been completed, but before the former Town Hall had been demolished and the Royal Exchange extended. The lower illustration shows Cross Street on a quiet Sunday morning in the late 1970s. Many of the buildings shown in the top photograph existed then and still do today.

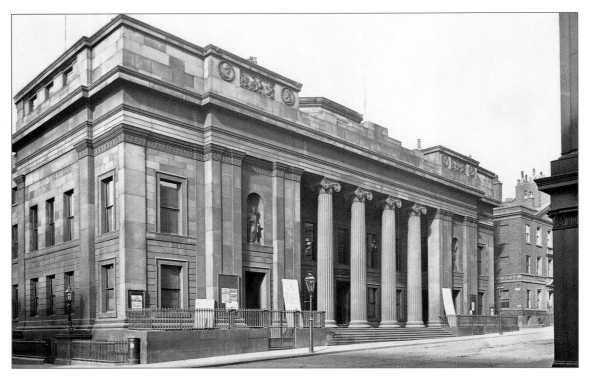

Until 1838 Manchester was governed jointly by the Court Leet and Police Commissioners, first appointed in 1792. Originally, the Police Commissioners had offices on Police Street, but in time, these premises became unsuitable. A new building known as the Town Hall was built on the corner of Cross Street and King Street on the site of Dr Charles White's house. Designed by Francis Goodwin at a cost of £29,000, it consisted of

offices for the Deputy Constable and the Police Commissioners, separated by a large hall suitable for public meetings and concerts. In 1838, when Manchester became a borough, the Police Commissioners refused to accept the legality of the new borough and refused to hand over the Town Hall. Eventually, they accepted the inevitable and the building was transferred to the Borough Council.

When the City Council moved to the Town Hall in Albert Square, the former Town Hall was taken over and adapted for Manchester Free Library's reference department as their former building on Byrom Street had been declared unsafe and closed. The Reference Library continued to use the building until 1912 when a structural survey revealed that it was becoming dangerous. As a result, the reference library was closed and transferred to temporary huts in Piccadilly, which it occupied until 1934. The former Town Hall was demolished, the columns of the portico being re-erected at Heaton Park, and the site sold. In its place a branch of Lloyds Bank was built, adding to the variety of architectural styles in central Manchester.

The decision to build a new Town Hall was taken in 1863 as the original building was inadequate for the growing functions that Manchester City Council was taking on, but it was some years before a site was agreed. A competition to find a suitable design was then organised. The winner was Alfred Waterhouse, who went on to design several other buildings in Manchester over the next three decades. Work started in 1868 and was completed in 1877. The new building was in complete contrast to the classical style of the original Town Hall as it was in the Gothic style, the fashion of the time. The first meeting of the City Council was held in the building in February 1877 (although parts of it had been occupied two years earlier). It had been hoped that Queen Victoria might open the building, but she declined the invitation and so the official opening was conducted by the Mayor, Alderman Abel Heywood, in September 1877. This photograph was taken in the early 1970s as the trees in Albert Square were becoming established.

King Street is a street of two distinct halves. The section between Cross Street and Deansgate is narrow and devoted to shopping whereas the part between Cross Street and Spring Gardens, shown here in the 1960s, is wider and devoted to finance. The smoke-blackened buildings on the left were erected in the mid-19th century. The one closest to Lloyds Bank was built for the District Bank on the site of the York Hotel. Next to it was a building constructed by the Royal London Insurance Co. in 1862 and leased to Vulcan Insurance, which eventually purchased it. Both buildings were demolished in the 1960s. Also visible are the Reform Club and, in the background, several banks which were built in the last decades of the 19th century. (*Chetham's Library*)

With the demolition of the District Bank and Vulcan Insurance buildings, two new buildings were added to King Street. The District Bank, which had become part of the National Westminster Bank, was replaced by an imposing multi-storey building designed by Casson, Conder & Partners and completed in 1969. The black cladding contrasts with the white Portland stone of the adjacent Lloyds Bank. The building erected on the site of the insurance offices is a much 'lighter' building with extensive use of glass to create an airy appearance. (*D. Brearley*)

In the early 1720s there was a proposal to build a new church in central Manchester, but nothing was done until 1753 when an Act of Parliament authorised one to be built on land belonging to the Collegiate Church behind Deansgate. The design of the new church, dedicated to St Mary, was said to have been based on that of Knutsford parish church. It was completed in 1756. Originally there was a steeple and a gilt ball and cross on top of the tower, but in the 1820s strong winds damaged the cross and ball and they were taken down. Further storm damage in the 1830s resulted in the steeple being removed, leaving just the tower, which can be seen in the picture on the right, taken about 1888. During the 19th century the church began to suffer from declining congregations as the increasing number of business premises reduced the numbers who lived in the city centre. Eventually, it was decided that it was no longer viable to retain the church, so it was demolished. The graveyard, which was said to contain over 20,000 burials, was landscaped and converted into Parsonage Gardens (bottom). (*Modern photograph by D. Brearley*)

Although improvements were made to the south side of Deansgate in the 1860s, little was done to improve the north side until the 1890s when some of the older properties were demolished and replaced by new buildings, as this view of *c.* 1910 shows. It also shows the piecemeal nature of the development as the building at the corner of Deansgate and St Mary's Street and Haywards, the china and glass merchants, had both been built in the middle of the 19th century to what appears to be a new building line. There was more redevelopment when Diocesan House (built in 1910) replaced the low-rise building next to the Midland Bank and further change when the Deansgate Cinema was built in 1914; after the Second World War a new Co-op store was erected on the site of the Deansgate Arcade. Today, some of these buildings have been adapted to suit modern requirements. The idea of sitting on the pavement and having a drink was alien to Manchester residents in the 19th century, but today it is acceptable: witness these people having a drink outside a building that was put up in the 1950s for the Co-op.

When Deansgate was widened in the 1860s one of the new buildings was Barton Buildings, named after the then owner of the site. The centrepiece was a cast-iron and glass shopping arcade known as Barton Arcade, designed by Corbett, Raby & Sawyer and completed in 1871. The Deansgate façade of the building gives little indication of the arcade's splendour. At street level there are shops, although when it opened there was criticism that the windows were too large to be properly dressed. The upper floors were used as offices while at the very top a flat was provided for a caretaker. In the 1980s the arcade was extensively refurbished and again, after the IRA bomb, further restoration took place. Today, it is admired as one of the architectural gems of Victorian architecture in Manchester and in many respects could be said to be the precursor of the modern covered shopping area. (*D. Brearley*)

From Market Street to Smithfield

After the Second World War there was an urgent need to replace
buildings that had been destroyed or damaged in the blitz. Sometimes
this involved individual buildings, but in some areas wholesale
redevelopment was needed as the future role of the city centre was
considered. One such area lay between Market Street, Corporation
Street, Withy Grove/Shudehill and High Street, and became the site of
the Arndale Centre. The redevelopment involved the demolition of
many buildings and the closure of streets like Brown Street, which
originally linked Cannon Street with King Street. When the Arndale
Centre was planned, the portion of Brown Street between Cannon
Street and Market Street, shown here in the late 1960s, was closed and
the buildings along its length demolished.

It was not until 1846 that the first part of Corporation Street was completed as far as Withy Grove. In 1850 the complete length of Corporation Street was opened, thus providing an improved link between York Street (now Cheetham Hill Road) and central Manchester. Within a short period the junction of Cross Street, Corporation Street and Market Street became very busy, so much so that by the beginning of the 20th century policemen had to be

placed on point duty to ensure the smooth running of the traffic. This photograph from 1914 shows horse-drawn vehicles and electric trams all mixed together while pedestrians tried to cross the road safely. All that's missing is the motor car and motorised lorry, both of which had begun to make their appearance in increasing numbers by this time.

In the latter half of the 20th century the gradual pedestrianisation of Market Street reduced the congestion at the junction of Cross Street, Corporation Street and Market Street. However, it is only since 1996 and the prohibition of traffic (except buses) along parts of Cross Street and Corporation Street that this junction became considerably less crowded, as the photograph shows. In the background is the modernistic bridge linking the Arndale Centre with the Marks & Spencer building; this replaced the original bridge erected in the 1970s and destroyed in the 1996 explosion. Another result of the bomb blast was that the owners of the Arndale Centre took the opportunity to improve the external appearance of the building, which had always been subject to criticism and even ridicule on occasions. Instead of a solid wall of yellow tiles along the Corporation Street frontage and the bridge over Market Street, glass panels were introduced to lighten the appearance of the building. On the corner of Market Street and Corporation Street, instead of a plain right-angled corner, the opportunity was taken to introduce brickwork into the façade, along with a corner turret.
(D. Brearley)

Market Street was originally known as Market Stede Lane. During the 17th and early 18th centuries the street gradually extended southwards towards Piccadilly, but little regard was paid to the building line so that its width varied considerably. As Manchester grew in size and importance, so Market Street became increasingly congested and dangerous. In 1820 it was decided to widen the road and reduce the gradient. This engraving dates from 1820, just before work started. It shows how steep the street actually was and its variety of widths. By 1835 all but one of the old buildings had been cleared and replaced at a cost in excess of £300,000, all raised from the rate-payers.

The widening of Market Street marked the beginning of a change in its character. Until the 1820s many of the buildings were shops with residential accommodation on the upper floors, but the new buildings tended to be more commercial with the upper floors being used as offices, workrooms or for storage. During the latter half of the century further changes took place when buildings erected in the 1820s and '30s were replaced by buildings that were in keeping with the needs and style of the late 19th century. This image shows Market Street looking towards the Royal Exchange in the 1930s. Walk down Market Street today and note how many of these buildings still remain, although the shop fronts have been altered.

Market Street in the mid-1970s, when it was half-way between the road being crowded with traffic and full pedestrianisation. Already, the Arndale Centre is completed and work had commenced on the refurbishment of some of the buildings on the left-hand side. The absence of buses suggests that these too have been banned, enabling pedestrians to wander across the road in comparative safety.

Market Street in 2001, now completely free from traffic. Where cars, buses, trams, lorries and vans used to run, there are market traders and people trying to undertake surveys. The idea of creating a traffic-free Market Street was first proposed in the early 1900s, but nothing came of this until the 1970s when a start was made in reducing the amount of traffic using the road; pedestrianisation was finally achieved in 1986. This view of Market Street is similar to the previous three, with the results of rebuilding the bridge across the road visible in the form of more glass being used than had previously been the case. (*D. Brearley*)

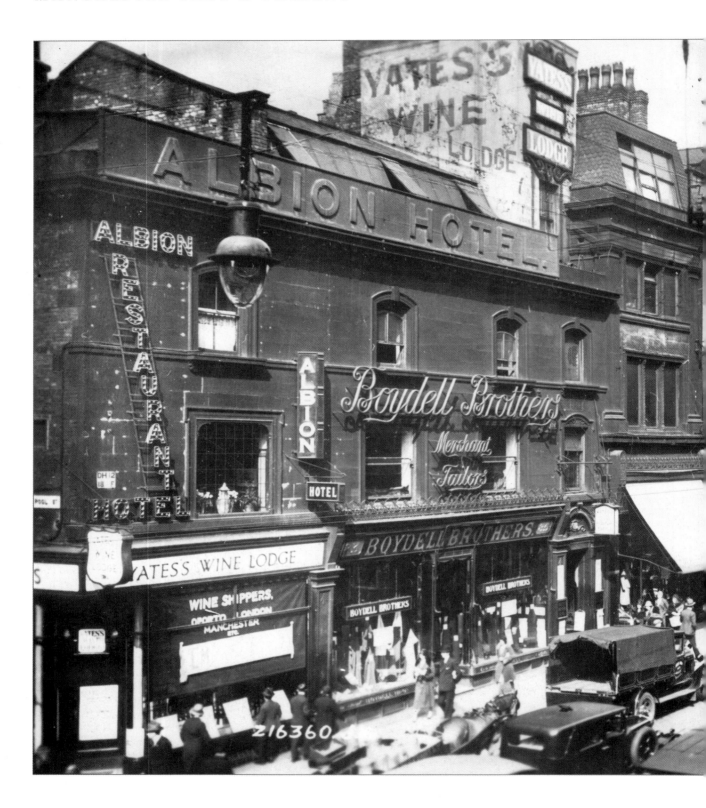

Market Street, Manchester.

This view of Market Street was taken in the mid-1930s and shows some of the buildings which were demolished when the Arndale Centre was constructed in the 1970s. Among the buildings seen here is the Market Street cinema (just to the left of the left-hand tram), which was built in the 1930s on the site of Palace Buildings. This cinema had a varied history and was known by several names until it was closed in the 1970s, its last name being the Cinophone. Another well-known Manchester institution can also be seen, Yates's Wine Lodge, which appears to have occupied the ground floor of the Albion Hotel. The Albion may have moved to this location in 1926 when its premises on the corner of Piccadilly and Oldham Street were acquired by Woolworths and demolished to enable Woolworths build a store in central Manchester. The tall building with the mast in the background belonged to John Rylands and Co., and is now occupied by Debenhams. All the buildings as far as the Rylands building were demolished to make way for the Arndale Centre.

During the late 1960s and '70s a large part of central Manchester was transformed by the construction of one of Europe's largest under-cover shopping areas, the Arndale Centre. In the process, one side of Market Street was cleared, together with property stretching from Corporation Street to High Street and as far as Withy Grove. Parts of this area were run down while some of the buildings required modernisation. There is no doubt that something needed to be done, and the type of development that took place was in keeping with 1960s architectural concepts. The new Arndale Centre included branches of various multiple shops such as W.H. Smiths, Littlewoods, Dixons and C&A as well as a number of smaller, specialist retailers and a market to replace the retail market formerly located at Smithfield. Coupled with the building of the Arndale Centre, discussions were held about closing Market Street to through traffic, which was eventually achieved in 1986. The 1996 bomb resulted in serious damage to the Corporation Street end of the Arndale Centre, but the owners took the opportunity to make improvements both internally and externally to the building. (*D. Brearley*)

In the early 1820s a young merchant, John Rylands, arrived in Manchester from Wigan to establish a branch of a firm that had been trading successfully in his home town for a number of years. He acquired a site on New High Street where he opened a warehouse from which he supplied the home market with linen and cotton goods. Gradually the firm, then known as John Rylands & Sons, expanded into manufacturing as well as selling, their first enterprise being the manufacture of linen cloth. During the 1830s the emphasis changed from linen to cotton and then to cotton only. The partnership of John Rylands with his father and brothers broke up during the 1840s and John continued on his own, gradually expanding the warehouse in Manchester as well as acquiring cotton mills, bleachworks and printing works. During the 1850s the warehouse was rebuilt and covered a large part of the site between New High Street, High Street and Tib Street. When John died in 1888, he left around £2.5 million and a firm which claimed it could supply everything a person wanted from the cradle to the grave, with the exception of coal and food. By the 1880s the firm had expanded even further with its building now fronting Market Street, as the upper photograph of the early 20th century shows. It was replaced in 1931 by more modern premises as, by this time, the firm was also selling direct to the public. It is this building which was taken over by Pauldens in 1957 after their store on Cavendish Street had been destroyed by fire and which is now occupied by Debenhams.

As Manchester expanded in the 18th century several new roads were created including High Street, which linked Market Street, Cannon Street and Shudehill. Originally, it was lined with domestic buildings, but gradually these properties were replaced by warehouses. The left side of High Street was redeveloped several times by the Rylands firm, but the right side (shown here) was not affected until the decision was made to build the Arndale Centre. The new development involved the demolition of all the buildings between Market Street and Shudehill including those seen in this 1960s photograph, looking towards Market Street.

The construction of the Arndale Centre resulted in the demolition of the buildings shown above as the centre extended along High Street as far as Shudehill, being carried out over Cannon Street by means of a bridge. For much of its length along High Street the centre is devoid of any break in the yellow tiles, although where it turns into Market Street there are shops and shop windows, as this photograph of the corner shows. (*D. Brearley*)

The construction of Manchester's Metrolink tramway involved linking the railway lines which ran north and south from Victoria and Oxford Road stations. To do this the trams had to leave Victoria station and cross Manchester to reach Piccadilly before going along Mosley Street to meet up with the line to Altrincham from Oxford Road near Old Trafford. Although the tramlines ran along existing roads for most of their route through central Manchester, near Victoria station it was necessary to demolish a number of buildings and close several streets. One of the streets affected was Bradshaw Street, shown here in the early 1970s. This area had been one of the earliest to be developed as Manchester expanded in the mid-18th century and consisted of three-storeyed buildings with workshops on the upper floor. In addition, there were cellars that might originally have been used for residential purposes. In the 1970s the buildings retained their original workshop windows and several still had cellars, fenced off to prevent members of the public from falling into them. At the time these properties were occupied by small firms such as general warehousemen, electrical suppliers, shoe repairers and jewellers.

The demolition of the buildings on Bradshaw Street and the adjacent Snow Hill enabled trams to gain access from Victoria station to the road network. This demolition initially opened up new vistas of the CWS buildings on Balloon Street, Dantzig Street, Hanover Street and the rear of the buildings on Corporation Street, but the developments on the Printworks site have altered this. A Metrolink tram is seen approaching Shudehill along the line of Snowhill, while on the right is the entrance to Bradshaw Street, devoid of buildings. (*D. Brearley*)

The construction of the Arndale Centre meant the relocation of one of Manchester's traditional open air markets, selling second-hand books and records. This was located on Withy Grove, close to the Rovers Return public house, demolished in 1957. This 1930s photograph shows just how popular this market was, with customers hunting through piles of books for bargains. When the redevelopment started, the stalls were relocated to the corner of High Street and Church Street, but the number of stall-holders declined. Although it still exists today, records rather than books appear to be the main items traded.

One of the original routes into central Manchester from the east was along Shudehill and Withy Grove, where there were two of the city's oldest pubs, the Seven Stars and the Rovers Return, as well as larger properties such as Bradshaw Hall and smaller houses. In the early 19th century the removal of the markets to Smithfield ensured that this became a busy part of Manchester for most of the day. New buildings were erected during the 19th century, although some of the older ones managed to survive, as this photograph from the early 1970s shows. Many of these buildings were used as warehouses by some of the numerous small firms, often involved in the fancy goods trade, that have always existed in Manchester. Dominating the scene is the central service tower of the residential and office block of the Arndale Centre, while the builder's cabins are where the spiral ramp to the car park was later to be constructed.

The view today along the same road shows the effect the Arndale Centre and the construction of the Metro have had on the townscape. The service shaft in the photograph above has been surrounded by the completed building and many of the older buildings have been demolished. (*D. Brearley*)

This early 1970s view shows the top end of Shudehill with one of the few remaining buildings of the many which once stood there. This particular photograph is looking across the site which was formerly covered by one of the market buildings at Smithfield. The building in the front of the CIS tower was erected in the late 19th century for a firm which was involved in the manufacture and distribution of umbrellas. The demolition has opened up a new view across the northern part of central Manchester towards the CIS building, as well as providing an opportunity to see the buildings at the corner of Miller Street and Shudehill from a distance and to appreciate their architectural quality. Also visible, to the left of the CIS building, is the ventilation shaft of Strangeways Prison, opened in 1868.

In October 1851 Queen Victoria visited Manchester for the first time. Her route from Victoria Bridge to the Exchange was rather circuitous as it involved travelling along Shudehill and Swan Street before entering Oldham Street and returning to Piccadilly. Swan Street lies on the very edge of central Manchester with a mixture of buildings, the most impressive a market hall, opened in 1858 and shown below. As Swan Street linked the end of Rochdale Road with Great Ancoats Street, it was always very busy, as this 1930s photograph shows.

Not exactly the same view of Swan Street as above, but one which shows the former Market Hall, opened in 1858. When it was built, it was the beginning of a move by Manchester City Council to provide the market traders with better facilities. However, as shopping habits changed and the residential population of the surrounding area declined, so also did the markets. Eventually the Market Hall closed and since that time it has had a variety of uses including a job training centre for young people. (*D. Brearley*)

One of the busiest parts of the city was the Smithfield area with its various markets. It was bustling from early morning to late afternoon as not only were there market stalls which were patronised by members of the public but it was also the location of Manchester's wholesale fruit, vegetable and fish markets. From dawn deliveries would be made to every corner of the market in readiness for retailers to arrive to purchase their stocks for the day. This is the scene outside the retail fish market in June 1914; things have quietened down a little and the market porters are able to take a short break. The horse-drawn vehicles are probably waiting to be instructed where to go with their next delivery.

During the late 1960s and early '70s the wholesale markets were moved from the city centre to the site of the Manchester & Sheffield Railway Works in Gorton. The old market buildings then became redundant and new uses had to be found for them. Part of the retail fish and game market was demolished and the remainder converted into a craft centre. The roof of the whole fish market was taken off although the walls were retained, but no permanent use has yet been found for this imposing structure. The 1858 Market Hall has been retained, but the market building on the left of the upper photograph has been demolished. Recently, the area has been given a new lease of life as many of the old warehouses and offices in the area have been or are being converted into flats. The former shops along Thomas Street and Turner Street, which were once closely associated with the markets, have now become showrooms and warehouses for those selling textiles at local markets. This view shows what remains of the wholesale fish market, opened in 1878. (*D. Brearley*)

The corner of Pall Mall and Market Street on a busy Saturday afternoon, late 1960s. On the right a 1950s building houses a UCP shop and restaurant while on the left is part of the complex of buildings where the *Manchester Guardian* and *Manchester Evening News* were published until 1968, when both papers moved to Deansgate to share a building with the *Daily Mail*. In the distance are the offices of the recently completed National Westminster Bank on King Street.

Piccadilly

When the Esplanade at Piccadilly was created in 1853, it was regarded as a suitable location for a statue of Robert Peel. In 1856 another statue was erected on the Esplanade, that of the Duke of Wellington, seen here in the 1920s. The idea of putting up a statue to commemorate his achievements was suggested a fortnight after the Duke's death in 1852. Very quickly, £7,000 was raised and a competition organised to find a suitable design. The winner was Matthew Noble, who depicted the Duke standing as a political figure rather than on horseback as a military leader. The choice of design was not popular as the public wanted to commemorate his military rather than his political exploits, but when the statue was unveiled in front of a crowd estimated at around 100,000 it was received favourably as it paid tribute to both aspects of his life.

Manchester Infirmary was established in 1752 to provide treatment for those who could not afford to pay doctors. The original premises were in a rented house on Garden Street, off Withy Grove, but it was soon obvious that this was not going to be large enough. In 1753 the Trustees were offered a site on Lever's Row (now Piccadilly) which they accepted, and the new hospital was opened in 1755. It looked like a large Georgian house with two backward-projecting wings. It more than doubled the number of beds available to treat in-patients and also had facilities to treat out-patients. In 1765 the Lunatic Hospital and Asylum was built on the adjacent site, where it remained until 1845 when it moved to Cheadle. After the Lunatic Hospital left, the Infirmary took over its buildings, allowing extra beds to be added. This engraving shows the Infirmary and Lunatic Hospital and Asylum in the early 19th century before the original appearance of the buildings was altered.

During the 19th century the Infirmary was enlarged on several occasions, to meet the growing demand for treatment. In the mid-19th century there were no other general hospital facilities in Manchester to meet the needs of the poorer sections of the community and the growing number of industrial injuries. There were several specialist hospitals at the time and, in areas like Ardwick, Ancoats and Chorlton-on-Medlock, there were dispensaries that provided a limited range of treatment for local people. By the end of the 19th century Manchester Royal Infirmary had accommodation for around 270 patients and could have accepted more if there had been more beds. In the 1870s it had been suggested that the Infirmary should move to a 'greenfield' site on the edge of Manchester, but it was not until 1902 that this was finally agreed. The Infirmary, shown above, closed in 1908 when the new hospital opened and this building was demolished in 1910.

When it was decided that the Manchester Royal Infirmary should move, the new site chosen was on Oxford Road, close to the Royal Manchester Eye Hospital. The new building was completed in 1908 and incorporated all the latest developments such as X-ray facilities. There was also a considerable increase in the number of beds available for in-patients. The cost of the new hospital, which was £500,000, was met largely from the sale of the old site (£400,000) and from fund raising, as there was no government funding at that time. The new hospital was officially opened in 1909 by King Edward VII and Queen Alexandra, after whom two wards were named. This is the Infirmary shortly after it was opened and before the trees planted in front of it obscured the view.

When the Trustees of the Infirmary decided to move, they sold the Piccadilly site to the City Council, which had already decided that any future development should be restricted to the area covered by the existing buildings. After they had taken possession of the site, there was a debate in the local press about its use, but before any decision could be made it became necessary to erect temporary accommodation for the Reference Library whose premises had been declared unsafe. The library remained at Piccadilly until it moved to St Peter's Square in 1934. In the meantime the vacant site was landscaped and became known as Piccadilly Gardens. Recently the Gardens began to look run down and in 2000 they were closed and work started on a new building on the site, although it is said that part of the Gardens will be restored as a public open space. (*Modern photograph by D. Brearley*)

Until 1940 the backdrop to the Infirmary and later the Gardens was a range of warehouses, many of which were associated with the cotton industry. The top view shows three of these warehouses about 1930. The one on the left was occupied by the firm of Peel Watson & Co., 'warehousemen'. The second, with the name J. Templeton & Co. at the top, was technically on George Street and was known as Templeton House. It was occupied by a number of firms involved with textiles. The third warehouse was also in multi-occupation. The building on the left, in the Gardens, was an out-patients department which the Infirmary built when it left Piccadilly to provide for those who still worked and lived in central Manchester. In December 1940 many of these buildings were destroyed or severely damaged during the German blitz on the city. After the war the area between Parker Street and York Street, Portland Street and Mosley Street was subject to a major redevelopment that involved shops at street and first floor level with offices and a hotel (left). Work on the new development started in the late 1950s and the complex was finished over a decade later. Today, the Mosley Street end of the building together with Bernard House is being demolished in preparation for a new development on the site. (*Modern photograph by D. Brearley*)

During the interwar period traffic increased considerably in central Manchester. The growing number of buses in use, and parking between journeys in Piccadilly, began to cause serious problems. To resolve this, a one-way traffic system was introduced, but it did not solve the issue of the buses and trams parking around the area before their next journey. In 1931 it was decided that a bus station should be created on Parker Street, behind Piccadilly Gardens. Here, bus stands were erected giving some protection from bad weather. This late 1930s photograph shows passengers waiting for buses in Parker Street, sheltered from the rain by a canopy stretching the length of the bus station.

One of the areas that suffered a lot of damage in the Manchester blitz was Piccadilly. At Parker Street bus station many of the island bus shelters were destroyed and passengers were forced to wait in the open. This mid-1950s photograph shows the bus station with the only shelters next to Piccadilly Gardens. People waiting for buses which did not go from these stops had to queue without protection. Eventually, covered shelters were erected, but these gave the bus station a rather claustrophobic feel. Recently these bus shelters have been demolished and the bus station redesigned to give a more open feel while still providing passengers with protection from wind and rain.

Although one side of Piccadilly was dominated throughout the 19th century by the Infirmary, the opposite side presented an interesting range of buildings, some of which dated back to the late 18th century. This view of Piccadilly, from the early 1890s, shows the eastern side, looking from Market Street. The small building on the left is the Mosley Hotel, which moved to Piccadilly in about 1828 when it was displaced from Market Street. Shortly after the photograph was taken, the old building was replaced by a larger one to cater for the growing demand for hotel accommodation in the city centre. The building with the turret was one of Brooke Bond's shops. This firm was one of Manchester's most important purveyors of tea, blending its own tea and supplying other firms as well. The white building on the corner of Oldham Street was the Albion Hotel, replaced in 1926 by a Woolworths store. Further along, many of the lower-rise buildings have been rebuilt, but a number still remain today.

In the mid-19th century there was situated at the corner of Oldham Road and Piccadilly a hotel which one French visitor described as having a 'plain exterior' but one of the best cuisines in Europe. This is the front of the Albion Hotel in October 1901 as a huge crowd assembles to watch the unveiling of Queen Victoria's statue by Lord Roberts. According to the 1881 census returns, George Adami was the Albion's manager and there were eleven guests and thirty-one members of staff in the building that night. The Albion closed in 1926.

During the 20th century the use of many of the buildings on the eastern side of Piccadilly has changed. Bella Pasta now occupies the ground floor of the building that replaced the Mosley Hotel in the 1920s while the building occupied by Brooke Bond later became a jewellers and is now a building society office. Even Woolworths has closed, the result of a disastrous fire in the 1980s in which a number of people lost their lives. The tall building next to the former Woolworths was built in the 1920s and houses a bank. It was also home to the BBC until the 1970s. During the last decade several of the other buildings seen here have been replaced, although the overall character of this side of Piccadilly, with its shops and tall buildings, has been retained. (D. Brearley)

Tib Street runs from New Cross to Market Street and was long associated with the pet trade. It takes its name from the River Tib which flows under the road on its journey from Oldham Road to the River Medlock at Gaythorn. In the late 1960s, when this photograph was taken, there were buildings from several different periods to be seen on Tib Street, but some of the buildings have now been demolished. The church in the background is St Paul's, New Cross, designed by G.O. Scott and opened in 1875 as a replacement for St Paul's, Turner Street.

Tib Street, 2001. Many of the buildings still survive, although some are in need of refurbishment. At the end of the road the white building, formerly a piano shop and later a bank, remains, but the church has been demolished. The changing nature of the area is also reflected by the fact that the National Westminster Bank is now the National Bank of Pakistan. The area along Thomas Street and Turner Street, behind the photographer, has many wholesale clothing warehouses which supply market traders, many of whom come from India, Pakistan and Bangladesh. Just as in the past immigrant communities in Manchester made their living in the textile trade, so the same holds true today. (*D. Brearley*)

The first horse-bus service was introduced in Manchester by John Greenwood in 1824. Within a few years there were services to several parts of the town and the surrounding areas, encouraging those who could afford it to move away from central Manchester. A single journey cost 6*d*, which was too expensive for most people, but as the 19th century progressed fares gradually fell, making it easier for working people to travel by bus. The early horse-buses were drawn by two horses, but in 1851 a larger bus, which could carry more passengers, was introduced, requiring three horses to pull it. The top picture shows a horse-bus passing the Royal Hotel on Mosley Street in the 1890s on a route which had not been converted to horse-trams. Horse-drawn trams were introduced in 1877 and very quickly many of the horse-bus routes were converted to horse-tram operation. These new trams were said to be more efficient than horse-buses and could carry up to 42 passengers at a time at 7mph. With horse-trams came the introduction of workmen's fares, which were designed to help those who had moved to the suburbs and needed to travel to work. The middle photograph shows a horse-drawn tram on the Manchester to Openshaw route in front of the Infirmary towards the end of the 19th century. (*E. Gray*). In 1901 electric trams began to be introduced, run not by a private company, but by the city council. The early electric trams had open tops, but within a few years they were covered and windows introduced on the upper deck to protect passengers from the weather. The bottom picture shows electric trams in Piccadilly in about 1910.

During the 1920s there was a gradual switch from trams to motor-buses as it was felt that tramcars were one of the main causes of congestion in the city centre. War-time damage to the tram network resulted in a further reduction in the number of routes operated by electric trams. In January 1949 the last tram route was converted to motor-bus operation and trams became a thing of the past. This photograph shows one of Manchester Corporation's buses turning into Market Street.

In 1949 few people imagined that trams would reappear and become a vital part of the city's transport infrastructure, linking two separate railway lines. The main junction for the Metrolink network is in Piccadilly where trams from Bury, Altrincham and Eccles all meet. Although there are through trams from Bury to Altrincham, many of them go to Piccadilly station, as do all the trams to and from Eccles. This tram is heading for Victoria station and ultimately to Bury. The first stop it will encounter after leaving Piccadilly is just round the corner outside the former Lewis's store. (*D. Brearley*)

During the mid-19th century a large number of textile warehouses were erected for both the home and export trade. Although their external appearances were different, most followed a similar internal pattern in that the ground floor was up a flight of steps, enabling the basement to have some natural light. The offices were normally on the ground floor while the storage areas were on the upper floors. The main elevations of the building were usually of stone, or later terracotta, and presented an imposing appearance, but the rear of these warehouses was usually plain brickwork. The warehouses in this photograph stood between Aytoun Street and Minshull Street until the early 1970s when they were demolished. For many years they had been occupied by two firms of cotton goods manufacturers, J. F. &H. Roberts and Ashton Bros.

The Local Government Act of 1972 changed the face of English local government when it created metropolitan counties for the large urban conurbations. At the same time over 60 smaller councils in the area round Manchester were amalgamated to form 10 metropolitan district councils, changes which were not unanimously accepted by some communities. In 1974 this building, which replaced the buildings shown above, was acquired by the Greater Manchester County Council as its headquarters. In 1986 the GMCC was abolished and the building eventually became commercial offices used by several different firms. (*D. Brearley*)

Perhaps Manchester's best-known warehouse was that opened in 1858 by J. & S. Watts on Portland Street. The building and site cost £100,000 and was designed by the architects Travis and Mangnall, with each floor said to be a different style of Renaissance architecture. In the early 20th century over 1,000 people were employed in the building. It was said that all orders received in the first post were despatched the same day. This early 20th-century photograph shows Watts Warehouse and another warehouse at the corner of Portland Street and Chorlton Street. The effect of these tall buildings, with similar ones across the road, was to give this part of Portland Street the appearance and feel of a canyon.

In the early 1970s Watts Warehouse was sold to a firm of property developers, but the economic crash of the mid-1970s and falling property prices resulted in the firm going bankrupt. The receivers wanted to demolish the building, but this caused a huge public outcry and permission was refused. Eventually, the building was sold and converted into the Britannia Hotel. Many of the internal features have been retained although not all are visible to the guests staying there. Across the road, behind the buses, is the building erected in the late 1960s and early '70s for the Bank of England's Manchester branch, beyond which is Piccadilly Plaza and above it the Piccadilly Hotel. (*D. Brearley*)

In the late 19th century the part of Oldham Street near Piccadilly was regarded as a mecca for ladies. It was where the main haberdashery and ladies' fashion shops were located as well as Affleck and Brown's store. This early 20th-century illustration shows how busy Oldham Street was then. Among the shops were Goodsons (mantle manufacturers), Foster & Sons (trimmings dealers), Lowes (drapers) and mantle makers Alfred Steindall and Robert Lomas. For ladies in need of a new servant, there was even a servants' registry at 6 Oldham Street (on the right).

During the second half of the 20th century Oldham Street gradually changed in character. The haberdashery shops disappeared and although stores like C&A made their appearance, the opening of the Arndale Centre attracted them away. Gradually, the quality of the shopping on Oldham Street declined as the centre of shopping moved in to Market Street and the Arndale Centre. So, although the buildings are the same, the nature of the street has changed since 1950. (D. Brearley)

Piccadilly is not just the area around the Gardens, it extends to the bottom of the approach to Piccadilly station. During the 19th century there were a number of hotels situated here including the Brunswick Hotel, the Imperial Hotel, the Hotel des Etrangers and the Waterloo Hotel. The Staff of the Hotel des Etrangers were fluent in various European languages. This was important as visitors from all parts of the world stayed in these hotels. The building with the flag is St Margaret's Chambers on Newton Street, which had been completed in 1892, not long before this postcard was produced.

Comparing this contemporary view with the one above, it will be seen that all the buildings on the left-hand side of this part of Piccadilly have been demolished and replaced by new ones. The oldest building still standing on this side of the road is the former Union Bank, built in 1909. The red brick building on the left is a modern extension to Hoyles Warehouse which has been restored and converted into a hotel. On the right-hand side of the road changes have been less dramatic, with many of the early 20th-century buildings still there today. (*D. Brearley*)

The original terminus of the Manchester & Birmingham Railway was at Bank Top, but in 1842 it moved to a new site at Store Street, which it was forced to share with the Manchester, Sheffield & Lincolnshire Railway. This led to bitter rivalry. As the level of passenger traffic increased the station became even more inadequate. Between 1860 and 1866 London Road station, as it became known, was rebuilt and enlarged. The new station included very carefully designated areas for both companies, a division that lasted well into the 20th century. This early 20th-century photograph shows the station and its approach. On the left, the MS&L built a series of warehouses which acted as an interchange between road, rail and canal transport as the Manchester terminus of the Ashton Canal was just behind the warehouses.

In 1958 the mid-19th-century office building at London Road station was replaced by a new office block and booking hall and the railway was electrified. The station was also renamed 'Manchester Piccadilly'. The train shed was left untouched although in 1999 it was refurbished, allowing passengers to see some of the fine iron-work used in its construction. Work has now started on improving the office block and the public areas to provide a station fit for the 21st century. The other major development to affect the setting of the station was the demolition of the MS&L warehouses. The replacement building, known as Gateway House, is sometimes described as looking like a 'lazy S' as it follows the curves of the station approach. (*D. Brearley*)

St Peter's Square & Albert Square

In 1794 a new church was consecrated on the western side of Manchester at the end of a new road linking the city centre with the Manchester and Wilmslow Turnpike in Chorlton-on-Medlock. The road was Oxford Street and the church, designed by James Wyatt, was dedicated to St Peter. Gradually, St Peter's Church became surrounded by houses and later by offices and warehouses. With the building of Central station, the population of the parish was significantly reduced so that by the beginning of the 20th century the church was struggling to survive. It closed in 1906 and was demolished the following year, the site becoming a traffic island that was subsequently landscaped. This view shows St Peter's Church in *c.* 1898 from Lower Mosley Street. On the extreme left of the picture are the remains of the Gentlemen's Concert Hall, demolition of which started in 1898 before the construction of the Midland Hotel.

Lower Mosley Street came into existence in the late 18th century as a continuation of Mosley Street. In the first half of the 19th century it was lined with houses and shops, which hid some poor quality areas from general view. This 1897 photograph shows the end of Lower Mosley Street as it approaches St Peter's Square. On the left are the Lower Mosley Street Schools, the People's Concert Hall and the Gentlemen's Concert Hall. These buildings were demolished in 1898 after the site was purchased by the Midland Railway Company to be used for the Midland Hotel. On the opposite side of the road there was a mixture of textile warehouses and smaller, domestic-scale properties (as can be seen on the right) and these were not demolished until the 1970s.

The demolition of the Gentlemen's Concert Hall, the People's Concert Hall and Lower Mosley Street Schools and their replacement by the Midland Hotel changed the appearance of this part of Mosley Street. Likewise, the demolition of St Peter's Church opened up the view along Mosley Street towards Piccadilly. It was not until the 1970s that the buildings on the south side of Lower Mosley Street were demolished, the site was used as a car park until a new hotel was built on it. (*D. Brearley*)

When the Lower Mosley Street Schools were demolished, the staff and pupils did not move far. A new building was erected nearby, where the schools were eventually to become the core of Manchester's Adult Education Service. The Education Department continued to use the buildings until about 1974 when it moved to new premises at All Saints, Chorlton-on-Medlock. The old buildings were demolished and the site used as a car park while the future development of the site was discussed.

Part of the site of the Lower Mosley Street Schools, together with the former Lower Mosley Street bus station, was eventually to be used for the construction of the Bridgewater Hall. There had long been a demand for a purpose-built concert hall in Manchester that was open to the public. When Charles Hallé started his orchestra in 1858 he used the Free Trade Hall, although he argued in favour of a dedicated concert hall in the centre of the town. Although others had made a similar point, it was not until the late 1980s that the decision was taken to build such a concert hall as a fitting home for the Hallé Orchestra, which is the oldest professional orchestra in the country and one of the oldest in Europe. The new hall was opened in 1996 and can be seen here with Hallé Square in the foreground. (*D. Brearley*)

In July 1880 the Cheshire Lines Committee opened its new station in central Manchester, appropriately named Central station. The new station provided facilities for the Manchester, Sheffield & Lincolnshire Railway, the Midland Railway, the Great Northern Railway and the Cheshire Lines Company itself. As well as services to Chester and London, the Cheshire Lines services to Liverpool rapidly gained a reputation for punctuality and regularity. They also introduced the concept of the cheap day return and rounded fares down so that payment could be made using a single coin if possible, which made booking easier for both the booking clerks and passengers. The station always looked unfinished as the office block planned for the front was never built. This picture of about 1910 shows the 210-foot span of the train shed area and the covered way erected to link the station to the rear of the Midland Hotel so that guests did not get wet walking between the station and their accommodation.

Central station closed in May 1969 and for a decade the future of the former station was in doubt as it passed through the hands of several different owners, some of whom used the station as a public car park. Eventually, the Greater Manchester Council and the private sector came together to convert the former train shed into a much-needed exhibition hall in the heart of Manchester. The new G-Mex Centre was opened in spring 1986 and has been used not only for exhibitions, but also for concerts and sporting events. More recently, conference facilities have been added at the side, thus increasing the use of the building and the site as a whole. (*Modern picture by D. Brearley*)

The Gentlemen's Concert Society was founded in 1770 by a group of amateur gentlemen flautists who wished to play together. They had some difficulty in finding a suitable location to rehearse and perform so they built a concert hall off Mosley Street. By the 1820s the hall was too small for the growing number of members who wanted to attend concerts so a new concert hall, designed by Richard Lane and said to have very good acoustics, was erected at the corner of Lower Mosley Street and Peter Street. It was here that Frederick Chopin played in 1848 and Felix Mendelssohn conducted *Elijah* a few years earlier. It was to perform with the society's orchestra that Charles Hallé came to Manchester in 1848 and was persuaded to stay on as the conductor. The last half of the 19th century saw a gradual decline in the fortunes of the Gentlemen's Concert Society and a growing need to undertake major restoration work on the building (left). In 1898 the Society sold the Concert Hall to the Midland Railway, which demolished it so that the Midland Hotel could be built.

The Midland Hotel was opened in 1903 on a site bounded by Windmill Street, Peter Street, Lower Mosley Street and Mount Street. Although the building might not appear so from the ground, it is almost triangular in shape as this photograph, of 1934 or early 1935, shows. When it opened, the hotel was regarded as one of the most luxurious in the country with all modern conveniences, including electric lifts for guests, several restaurants, a roof garden and its own orchestras to entertain the diners. This unusual view also shows the white glazed bricks used to reflect light in the centre of the triangle. Also visible is the dome of the main reading room of Manchester Central Library and the inside of the curtain wall that surrounds the dome and reading room.

One of the best-known buildings in central Manchester is the circular Central Library in St Peter's Square. The library was opened in 1934, replacing the huts in Piccadilly that had been the reference library's home for over two decades. The building of the library involved the demolition of a three-storeyed block which had been constructed in the mid-19th century. These properties, which can be seen behind the horse-drawn fire engine, looked like domestic dwellings, but housed offices, restaurants and small workshops.

Manchester's Central Library not only houses the city's main reference library, but also a general lending library and several specialist departments covering commercial information, a technical library, a language and literature library, an arts library, the Henry Watson Music Library and the local studies department. In addition, it is also the administrative headquarters for Manchester Public Libraries and the Library Theatre. Members of the public only see a small percentage of the books on open access as the library has many thousands of other books together with archival material and manuscripts housed in around 40 miles of shelving on four stacks under the main circular reading room. When the library opened, the printed word was all-important, but as the 20th century progressed microfilm and microfiche material became available and now information can be obtained electronically over the Internet. Things have come a long way since Edward Edwards opened the first public library in the country in Manchester under the terms of the 1850 Public Libraries Act in September 1852. (*D. Brearley*)

Oxford Street, constructed in the 1790s, provided a direct link between the villages south of Manchester and the town centre. In the late 19th century Oxford Street was regarded as the entertainment centre of Manchester as there were several theatres located along its length. These included the Prince's Theatre, the St James's Theatre and Hall, the Palace of Varieties and the Hippodrome. This view shows Oxford Street around 1937 shortly before the one-way system was introduced (which meant that all traffic coming into Manchester had to travel along Oxford Street and had to go out via Princess Street). In the late 1990s the section of Oxford Street between St Peter's Square and Portland Street has reverted to two-way traffic again. The photograph shows the increasing amount of motor traffic trying to squeeze between the trams and the pavement. The building behind the third tram in the queue is the Prince's Theatre, which was opened in 1864 to encourage revivals of Shakespeare's plays. It closed in 1940 and was to be converted to a cinema, but bomb damage prevented this. Just behind the front building on the left is the Odeon Cinema, opened in 1932 as the Paramount, and beyond that the Plaza dance hall.

This is a similar view to the one above, taken from street level in 2001. Many of the buildings have been replaced by modern structures. The site of the former Prince's Theatre is now Peter House while on the opposite side of the road, the former Plaza dance hall site is covered by a new hotel. Some of the buildings, like the Odeon Cinema and further along, Churchgate House and St James's Buildings, are still there today. It is still possible to recognise the Oxford Street of 63 years ago despite all the changes that have taken place. The trams have been replaced by buses, and the number of private vehicles has dramatically increased in the intervening years. (*D. Brearley*)

On 16 December 1904 a new variety theatre opened on Oxford Street – the Hippodrome. Designed by Frank Mitcham for Oswald Stoll, the building incorporated a sliding roof over the auditorium to increase ventilation, an area which could be filled with water for 'water spectaculars', and stalls and cages under the stage for performing animals. When the Hippodrome closed in February 1935 the name and the revolving sign from the roof were transferred to the Ardwick Empire, which was renamed the Ardwick Hippodrome. The building was partially rebuilt and converted into a cinema and was to be known as the Granada, but a few weeks before it opened it was acquired by Gaumont-British and renamed the Gaumont. The new cinema cost £300,000, had 2,500 seats and was said to be the most luxurious in Manchester. It was opened by Jessie Matthews and her husband Sonny Hale. The first film was Alfred Hitchcock's *The 39 Steps*, starring Robert Donat and Madeleine Carroll. The foyer of the cinema ran the full length of the building while its Long Bar became a popular haunt of GIs during the Second World War. After the war the Gaumont was used as a 'showcase' cinema for 70mm films such as *South Pacific*, which had long runs in Manchester. The Gaumont closed in 1974, was converted to a nightclub (closed in 1991) and shortly afterwards the building was demolished. The new building on the site is a multi-storey car park. (*Modern photograph by D. Brearley*)

Late 19th-century Manchester had several theatres where plays, pantomimes and opera could be staged, but no variety theatre. The St James's Theatre, opened in 1884 as 'the home of heavy drama', survived until 1909 when it was converted into a cinema which closed in 1911. Five years after the St James's opened, plans were announced for a variety theatre on the adjoining site, where the four-storeyed buildings can be seen in the picture. This new theatre was to be called the Palace of Varieties and was built on an island site at the corner of Whitworth Street and Oxford Street. The Palace opened in 1892.

When the Palace of Varieties opened, the management concentrated on variety or vaudeville acts, often starring leading artists of the day. In 1913 the building was extensively refurbished to meet competition from other places of entertainment. After the First World War the Palace replaced its variety programmes with a mixture of straight plays, musicals, pantomimes and revues. The decline in interest in live theatre brought about by competition from television after the Second World War and rivalry from the Opera House forced a radical re-think as to whether there should be two large theatres in central Manchester. It was decided that there should not and so the Opera House was closed, but not before the Palace was refurbished. However, it was soon discovered that certain productions could run for long periods and still attract audiences so the Opera House was reopened to cater for longer-running shows while the Palace concentrated on shorter runs. (*D. Brearley*)

In 1790 a new hospital was founded dedicated to helping pregnant women and babies. It was known as St Mary's Lying-in Hospital and was located in a former house close to old Salford Bridge. During the first half of the 19th century the hospital had several different locations in both Manchester and Salford, but in 1856 it was decided that it was necessary to have a purpose-built hospital. The new building, erected on Quay Street at a cost of £4,300, had between 80 and 90 beds of which 25 to 30 were planned for use by small children and babies. The new hospital was subject to much criticism in its early days. Among the complaints were dirty kitchens, poor quality food and lack of privacy. During the 1880s the population of the area around Quay Street gradually declined while the move of Owens College to Chorlton-on-Medlock affected the relationship between the hospital and the medical school at the college. There was also a feeling that the hospital was not in a prominent position and therefore tended to be overlooked. The result was the decision to move to a new site at the corner of Oxford Street and Whitworth Street West. The new building, which cost £30,000, was designed by Alfred Waterhouse and dominated the junction of the two roads (top). In 1910, after a merger with the Southern Hospital for Women and Children, St Mary's moved some of its facilities to a new hospital on Hathersage Road. The Whitworth Street building remained open until the 1960s when the services it provided were transferred to the Hathersage Road. The old building was eventually demolished and the site used as a car park until 2000 when work started on erecting apartments on the site (bottom). (*D. Brearley*)

Princess Street as far as Portland Street was originally known as David Street. In the mid-19th century it was renamed Princess Street as it was extended to link with Upper Brook Street. The earliest part developed was at its junction with Cooper Street, where the doorway to one of these 1790s houses can be seen on the extreme left. From the mid-19th century onwards Princess Street became lined with textile warehouses, each with its own particular style. One feature common to all of them was the location of the chimneys, which were always on an outer wall to reduce fire risk. This can be seen very clearly on the warehouses in the centre. It should be noted that insurance companies insisted on this, otherwise premiums were increased. This view of the junction of Princess Street and Mosley Street was taken from the junction of Cooper Street and Princess Street in the early 1970s. The block on the left had been erected in the latter half of the 19th century and consisted of shops at street level and offices or workshops above. Part of the site had originally been used for the building which housed the Manchester Mechanics Institute between 1825 and 1853, when it moved to 103 Princess Street. The light-coloured building partially masked by the no. 50 bus was erected in 1870 to the designs of Clegg and Knowles. Today it has been converted into a hotel, a trend which was started in the 1870s when Collie's warehouse on Aytoun Street became the Grand Hotel.

The trees on the right of the top picture are where the buildings on the right were once located. The site was acquired by Manchester City Council with the intention of building a second extension to the Town Hall on it. However, changes in local government in the early 1970s coupled with restrictions on local government expenditure meant the scheme was shelved. The site was landscaped and became known as the Peace Garden (centre). Before the trees were established, the open space presented an attractive view of Charles Barry's Art Gallery (bottom) and, looking the other way, of the Central Library, Town Hall Extension and the Midland Hotel. (*D. Brearley*)

When Prince Albert died in 1862, Manchester honoured his memory with an impressive memorial designed by Thomas Worthington and including a statue of the Prince given by Alderman Goadsby. The memorial was erected in a newly created square where previously there had been several workshops, a coffee roasting works and back-to-back housing. On one side of the new square was the Town Yard, where the Town Hall was eventually built, while the opposite side was lined with the shops, warehouses and offices seen above. Many of these buildings housed shipping companies that had established a presence in the city after the opening of the Manchester Ship Canal in 1894.

Over the years the paved area in Albert Square has been increased so that it is no longer possible to drive in front of the Town Hall. In 1968, to mark its centenary, the *Manchester Evening News* planted a number of trees which have gradually come to maturity. The result is that it is not now possible to get a similar view of the buildings facing the Town Hall as in the top picture. The buildings shown above were demolished in the 1960s and replaced by modern office buildings designed to be in keeping with the architecture of the surrounding buildings. Part of the range of buildings can be seen here while in the Square, the publicity vehicle for the 2002 Commonwealth Games appears to be attracting some considerable interest. (*D. Brearley*)

The development of a town often results in physical features being lost so that names of streets mean little to people in the late 20th and early 21st centuries. A case in point is Mount Street, which runs from Albert Square to Windmill Street. This road leads gently uphill towards the site of G-Mex, where the land drops away sharply to the valley of the River Medlock. One of the earliest buildings on Mount Street was the meeting house of the Society of Friends, the gateposts and railings of which can be seen on the left of this photograph taken in about 1878 on what appears to be a very quiet day, possibly a Sunday afternoon, as the Town Hall clock indicates it is 2 p.m. The tall building on the left is known as Lawrence Buildings and was constructed for the Inland Revenue. The buildings on the opposite side of Mount Street were demolished when the Town Hall Extension and Central Library were erected in the 1930s. In the background, Albert Square is just visible with the Albert Memorial in the centre.

Mount Street in 2001 with the gateposts of the Friends Meeting House still visible although the railings have disappeared. Lawrence Buildings has also survived the passage of time although no longer used by the Inland Revenue. It is on the opposite side of the road that the greatest changes are visible. The attractive Victorian buildings have been replaced by Vincent Harris's Town Hall Extension, completed in 1938, while on the extreme right is Manchester's Central Library. The road has also been narrowed as the demand for parking has increased. (*D. Brearley*)

One of Manchester's most familiar buildings is the Free Trade Hall on Peter Street. Built in 1856, it has been the venue for concerts, plays, public meetings, exhibitions, boxing matches and school speech days. In 1996, with the opening of the Bridgewater Hall, the building became redundant and attempts were made to find a new use for it. The original 1856 building was severely damaged in the Manchester blitz so all that remains are the Peter Street and South Street outer walls. The remainder of the building and the interior all date from the early 1950s when the hall was rebuilt. Various proposals have been tabled, but no decision yet has been made. (*D. Brearley*)

Peter Street came into existence in the early 1790s when Oxford Street was extended to meet a short road known as Yates Street, creating an alternative route from the south of Manchester to Deansgate and Castlefield. Although initially a street of private dwellings, it gradually became associated with the entertainment industry with the Theatre Royal, Gentlemen's Concert Hall, Free Trade Hall and the Folly or Tivoli Theatre to be found along its length. Peter Street was also the location of the Swedenborgian Church in Manchester, which had been established in 1793 at the Deansgate end of the street. The New Jerusalem Church also provided education for boys and girls from its congregation and the surrounding area. The church moved to Whalley Range in the 1880s and the buildings were taken over by the Trustees of the Whitworth Institute as a school for teaching spinning and weaving. Eventually the Institute became part of the Manchester Municipal College of Technology. The site was acquired by the Manchester and Salford Methodist Mission which built the Albert Hall on the site partly as a church and partly as a centre where those working in the entertainment industry in the area could relax without having to spend their free time in the pub. One such place of entertainment was the Grand Pavilion in the upper picture, which was opened in 1883. After 1893 it began to stage traditional variety acts together with circus and other novelty acts. It was converted into a cinema in 1916 and closed in 1924, the building being converted into a reading room of the Christian Science Church. Now both former churches are places of entertainment. (*Modern picture by D. Brearley*)

In the last two or three years the Deansgate end of Peter Street has undergone a dramatic transformation. The former railway offices that masked the Great Northern Railway Warehouse have been demolished and replaced by leisure facilities. The warehouse itself, built in 1895, has been made into a car park, thus preserving one of the great railway structures of Manchester. These three photographs show the offices that were demolished, the pub that has replaced them on Peter Street and the piazza behind where people can sit and enjoy a drink or conversation. (*Modern pictures by D. Brearley*)

Castlefield

Outside railway stations was always a good location for newspaper sellers as passengers arriving at or leaving the station tend to want a paper. This newspaper seller is located on Whitworth Street West, across the road from Knott Mill (now Deansgate station).

Whitworth Street West was created in the late 19th century when Manchester began a programme of improving some of the roads around the city centre. Around this time Gloucester Street was renamed Whitworth Street West and extended towards Deansgate and Castlefield. The area where the new Whitworth Street West was to go was one of poor-quality housing sandwiched between the Rochdale Canal, on the left, and the Manchester, South Junction & Altrincham Railway line on the right. At the same time as the slums were being cleared, the railway company was persuaded to improve Knott Mill station, which included building a new entrance and booking office, completed in 1896. (*Manchester Local Studies Unit*)

Whitworth Street West and its junction with Deansgate in 2001. The Railway Hotel on the left of the picture above has disappeared and in its place is a flight of steps leading to the Metro station. Knott Mill station, now renamed Deansgate station, is still recognisable, but across the road is a footbridge. This was constructed in the mid-1980s to provide a direct link for passengers wanting to transfer from British Rail's trains to the Metrolink tram system or vice versa. It also provides a route for pedestrians to the G-Mex Centre. (*D. Brearley*)

Liverpool Road came into existence as a street in the 1790s and was given its present name in about 1806 when Regent Road Bridge across the River Irwell resulted in improved access to the main road to Liverpool. The road is perhaps best known for the fact that at the northern end of it the Liverpool & Manchester Railway built its Manchester terminus in 1830. This 1896 view shows the Deansgate end of the street with its three-storeyed houses and shops that date from the 1790s. When this photograph was taken there were several shops which were occupied by 'furniture brokers', who were second-hand furniture dealers, as well as shops selling meat, green-grocery and several shops occupied by ladder makers. (*Manchester Local Studies Unit*)

Although Liverpool Road has changed over the years and many of the houses which were to be found on the left-hand side of the road have been demolished, some remain at the Deansgate end. This photograph shows a few of them, including the White Lion public house. Several have been refurbished and lost some of their original features, but their survival is a reminder that Liverpool Road was once an important residential street. The trees beyond the White Lion are where the 1972 excavation of the Roman *vicus* or civilian settlement took place, which reawakened an interest in Roman Manchester and the Liverpool Road area. (*D. Brearley*)

In 1876 Manchester decided to stop having its traditional fair which had been held since 1222. The fair had moved to Liverpool Road in 1823 and had spread throughout the surrounding streets causing tremendous problems for those living and working in the area. At the same time the council also wanted to build a market hall nearby for the people who lived in the Castlefield area. As they could not construct a building of the size they felt was necessary because of the existence of St Matthew's Church, two separate buildings were erected, the Upper Campfield Market, shown here *c.* 1902, and the Lower Campfield Market, just visible in the distance. Both buildings were opened in the early 1880s, but were not successful in attracting the traders that the council hoped would move into the new buildings. The local people still preferred to go over to Smithfield for their shopping, so the buildings were something of a white elephant. The Upper Campfield Market tended to be used by second-hand clothes dealers and similar traders while the Lower Campfield Market was converted into an exhibition hall, City Hall, in the 1920s. Even today, there are problems with finding a permanent use for the Upper Campfield Market. (*Manchester Local Studies Unit*)

This is the other former market building which was originally known first as Lower Campfield Market and then City Hall. In appearance the two buildings are very similar in that they consist of a cast-iron frame, a glass roof and originally had open sides. Whereas there have always been difficulties finding a use for the Upper Campfield Market building, there has been no such problem with this one. For many years in the 20th century it was used as an exhibition hall and when it ceased to be used for that purpose, it was converted into an Air and Space Museum. Today, it forms the Air and Space Gallery of the Museum of Science and Industry, Manchester. (*D. Brearley*)

Until 1952 Liverpool Road was the location of what was described as 'one of the finest Gothic spires in Lancashire'. The spire was that of St Matthew's Church. Designed by Charles Barry, who later designed the Art Gallery and several other buildings in Manchester, it cost £14,000, which was paid out of a fund established by the government to build new Anglican churches in the growing industrial towns. St Matthew's Church was consecrated in 1825 and in 1851 served a population of over 10,000, who a few years earlier had been described by a student as 'heathen'. During the latter half of the 19th century the population began to decline so that in 1906 St Matthew's was one of the churches listed to be closed at some unspecified date in the future. The closure took place in the 1930s and the building, after being used in the war for barrage balloon and parachute manufacturing and packing, was demolished and a new office block erected on the site. These three illustrations show the church when it opened (top left), as it appeared between the wars (top right) and the replacement office block (left). (*Top right, Manchester Local Studies Unit; Modern photograph by D. Brearley*)

Liverpool Road station opened in September 1830 as the Manchester terminus of the world's first intercity passenger railway service. The station was used as a passenger station until 1844 when passenger services were transferred to Victoria station. Liverpool Road station was then turned into a goods station, a role in which it continued until 1975 when British Railways closed it down and sold the site to the Greater Manchester Council, which restored the original station building to be part of the Museum of Science and Industry in Manchester. The top photograph shows the station as it appeared *c.* 1904 with the original first-class entrance in the light-coloured part. The house at the corner of Liverpool Road and Water Street was built in about 1817 and was used by the goods agent. Later it was used as a car spares shop (centre), but when the site was acquired by the GMC the house was refurbished back to its original appearance. On the extreme left of the top photograph is the original bridge carrying the railway across Water Street. This was replaced in 1905 with the bridge that can be seen in the bottom photograph, which shows the restored station buildings. (*Modern photograph by D. Brearley*)

When Liverpool Road station became a goods depot in 1844, it was adequate for the amount of goods traffic the railway carried. During the 1850s freight increased rapidly and it became necessary to extend the site. About 1858 a new goods transfer shed was opened on the corner of Liverpool Road and Lower Byrom Street. This allowed road vehicles to drive straight into the building and unload on to a platform which was the same height as the bed of the cart and the railway wagon, making it easier to transfer goods between the two forms of transport. The top photograph shows this shed *c.* 1971 with a pile of goods waiting to be moved. When Liverpool Road goods station closed, this building was used to display locomotives at the 1980 Great Exposition organised to celebrate the 150th anniversary of the opening of the line. It was later converted into the Power Hall of the Museum where mill engines, railway engines and motor cars are displayed. (*Modern photograph by D Brearley*)

In 1769 a new church was consecrated on the edge of Manchester. It was built by Edward Byrom and was dedicated to St John (top). Within a short time new houses were built for those who wanted to live away from the centre of the city. In effect, these houses on St John's Street and Byrom Street became Manchester's first suburbs. In the late 18th century St John's attracted a fashionable congregation – so much so that St John's Street was nicknamed 'The Carriage Road to Heaven'. Gradually the area was engulfed by the expanding town and the residents moved away. St John's Church continued to provide for those who moved into the area, but as industry and commerce began to replace residential property, the congregation declined. In 1931 the church was closed and demolished, the site being converted partly into a children's playground (right) and a pleasant sitting area (bottom). Where the church once stood, a cross was erected recording the fact that over 20,000 people were buried in the churchyard, including John Owens, founder of Owens College, now Manchester University. (*Modern photograph by D. Brearley*)

Before canals were built, the Rivers Mersey and Irwell provided Manchester with its first bulk transport system using water. The rivers were improved to enable vessels of up to 50 tons to reach Quay Street, which was constructed to link the river with Deansgate. Gradually a series of warehouses were erected on the banks of the river where goods could be stored prior to being transported to Liverpool or to the warehouses and markets of Manchester. These warehouses were designed to enable goods to be moved easily from road to river or vice versa. This photograph, of about 1972, shows two of the Mersey–Irwell Navigation Company's warehouses on Water Street, known as the Victoria Warehouse and the Albert Warehouse.

The Mersey–Irwell Navigation was eventually taken over by the Bridgewater Canal, which was later incorporated into the Manchester Ship Canal Company. Gradually river traffic declined and the warehouses became redundant for their original purpose. They were used for a time for storage, but in the 1990s the Victoria Warehouse and the Albert Warehouse were converted into a hotel. The original window openings were retained while the doors which gave access to different levels for goods were replaced by plate-glass windows. This photograph shows the view across the entrance lock of the Manchester & Salford Junction Canal towards the converted warehouses. (*D. Brearley*)

During the postwar period the canal basins around Castlefield became very run down and the location of several scrap metal yards. To go through the area was not a pleasant experience as there were often fierce dogs roaming around, especially at weekends. This view, possibly from the late 1970s, shows the state of the area at that time with pallets and drums occupying one site, a damaged warehouse just visible under the railway arches and a workshop on the left. Dominating the area were the unused viaducts carrying the railway into the former Central station and Great Northern Warehouse and beyond them, the line to Altrincham and Liverpool. Little had been done to exploit the potential of this area at that time, but gradually all this was to change.

A view from almost the same angle as that above showing what has been achieved in the improvement of the canal basins in Castlefield in the course of the past two decades. The scrap yards have been removed, the canal basins opened up and the whole area given a make-over with new bridges and buildings. People wander around the area looking at this important aspect of Manchester's transport heritage in a way that would have been impossible 20 years ago. (*D. Brearley*)

The corner of Potato Wharf and Liverpool Road, late 1970s. During the 19th century there had been a number of ladder manufacturers on Liverpool Road, several of them from the Neild family. This small workshop, with its tongue-in-cheek name over the door, would have been typical of the type of small workshop that existed in this area during the 19th and early 20th centuries.

In the early 1980s the Manchester branch of the YMCA based on Peter Street discovered that it needed to spend a lot of money to restore its premises. At the same time the original purpose for which it had been established had changed and so it was decided to sell the building, together with Montgomery House in Whalley Range, and replace it with a hotel in Castlefield. The new building, shown above, was built at the corner of Potato Wharf and Liverpool Road and incorporated a swimming pool and other leisure facilities as well as accommodation.
(*D. Brearley*)

During the 1960s and '70s the land behind Potato Wharf was used to manufacture concrete using materials brought into Liverpool Road goods depot. The equipment used for this is visible behind Jacob's Ladders, opposite. When this industrial use ceased, it became possible to redevelop the arms of the Bridgewater Canal that entered the Staffordshire Warehouse, demolished in the early 1950s. The result was the creation of the Castlefield Arena, overlooked by the rear of the Castlefield Hotel (top). The Arena (right) is used for a variety of events including concerts and the annual Castlefield Carnival. Large crowds gathered here in September 1993 to await the decision on which city was to host the 2000 Olympic Games. (*D. Brearley*)

In 1764 the Bridgewater Canal reached Castlefield where it divided into two arms. One went towards Deansgate and was used by boats bringing coal into Manchester from Worsley. The coal, carried in small containers, was raised to street level by a water-powered hoist. This part of the canal was where the earliest warehouses, the Duke's and the one now known as the Grocers' Warehouse, were built. The other arm, shown here, went towards Liverpool Road and what is now the Castlefield Arena. The whole area has received a facelift in the 30 years since the top photograph was taken. The railway bridges remain, but a footbridge across the canal has made access between the various parts of Castlefield much easier. Where there was once dereliction, trees now grow and visitors wander around looking at the canal and using the various bars and pubs that have been opened in the area. (*Bottom photograph by D. Brearley*)

These cottages, seen here in the early 20th century, survived until the mid-1960s when they were demolished. They were probably built in the late 18th or early 19th century for those who worked on either the Rochdale or the Bridgewater Canals, which meet under the bridge in the foreground. Looking at the area today, there appears to have been no room for this short terrace of cottages. The area has now been converted into a car park. (*Manchester Local Studies Unit*)

When the Bridgewater Canal was constructed there was no access between the canal and the River Irwell at the Manchester end. It was not until the Manchester & Salford Junction Canal Act was passed in 1835 that a lock was built between the two waterways. This photograph was taken *c.* 1974 when one of the last boats from Manchester docks to the Kellogg's factory in Trafford Park passed through the lock from the river on to the Bridgewater Canal. In the 1980s the lock was abandoned as a new link was made between the Bridgewater Canal and the Manchester Ship Canal at Pomona. It is now no longer possible to see this lock as it is boarded off.

One of the last warehouses to be built on the Bridgewater Canal was the Merchants' Warehouse. According to the datestone set in the stonework of the arches of the boat holes, the warehouse dates from 1825–6. As in all the other canal warehouses, small windows predominated, and heavy wooden beams carried the floors and the hoists to lift goods. In the early 1970s part of the warehouse was damaged by fire (left). The loss of part of the roof revealed the size of the timbers used in the construction of the building together with the pulley wheels that operated the hoists inside the building. After almost 20 years when nothing was done with the building, it has now been restored and converted into offices. The only major change to its appearance has been the conversion of the loading bay doors to windows and the provision of air conditioning and other services at the end of the building rather than on the roof. (*Modern photograph by D. Brearley*)

The Rochdale Canal was completed across Manchester in December 1804. One result was a reduction in the length of the journey from the east coast to Liverpool. At the same time the canal enabled factory owners in Rochdale and some of the West Yorkshire towns to have access to the ports of Liverpool and Hull. Although some traffic continued to use the canal well into the 20th century, stretches of it fell into disuse, including the 'Rochdale Nine' through central Manchester linking the Bridgewater Basin with the Rochdale Canal basin at Dale Street. This photograph, of January 1973, shows the derelict nature of the canal as it approached the Bridgewater Canal, devoid of water and with the skeletons of sunken boats lying on the canal bed.

During the 1980s pressure was brought to bear on the Rochdale Canal Company to do something about the stretch of the canal between Castlefield and Dale Street, especially as it provided a link between the Ashton and Peak Forest Canals and the Bridgewater Canal. The towpath was improved and the canal cleared of rubbish and refilled with water so that boats could travel through the heart of Manchester, while the towpath provides a pleasant walk from Castlefield to Princess Street, away from the traffic. As part of the improvement of the towpath, several new access points have been created. This photograph shows the transformation that has taken place with the timber yard shown in the top photograph having gone and the buildings on the right restored. (*D. Brearley*)

When the Mancunian Way was constructed in the 1960s and early '70s it terminated at a roundabout with Deansgate, by St George's Church. Very quickly this roundabout became a problem for vehicles using the Mancunian Way from the east side of the city trying to cross traffic leaving Manchester. This was solved by the construction of a flyover which took traffic heading to and from Deansgate over the roundabout. In the background is St George's Church, designed by Francis Goodwin and opened in 1828. As well as serving the people of Hulme, it was also used by the regiments based at the nearby Hulme Barracks.

When the Mancunian Way was extended in the 1990s to join up with Regent Road in Salford, it was carried under Chester Road, which removed the need for the flyover and it was subsequently demolished. This is the view today with traffic moving smoothly through the junction and over the Mancunian Way. It is still possible to join the Mancunian Way from all directions so the importance of this road as an inner city relief road has been maintained and will be increased when the final section of the inner city relief road is completed. The demolition of the flyover has also allowed St George's Church to be clearly seen again. This redundant church, after many false starts, is now being converted into flats. (D. Brearley)

And so to the Future . . .

During the late 1980s and early '90s Manchester made two unsuccessful attempts to bring the Olympic Games to England. However, the city did succeed in attracting the 2002 Commonwealth Games. This has involved the building of several new sporting facilities, two of which are located on former industrial sites on the eastern side of the city. In the 19th century east Manchester had become associated with engineering and mining. Surrounding the factories were a large number of terraced houses, which in the mid-20th century were earmarked for clearance. The gradual decline of the traditional employers of labour in the area and closure of factories had resulted in parts of east Manchester looking like an industrial wasteland. This photograph shows the area around the redundant Bradford Colliery around 1968 with partly demolished houses and a derelict industrial site, dominated by colliery pit-head gear.

The first of Manchester's new sporting facilities, the velodrome. To many people there was an element of surprise in building a national cycling centre in Manchester, but not to those who knew anything about sport in the city. For many years in the first half of the 20th century there had been a cycle stadium in Fallowfield, known as the Reg Harris Stadium. The new cycling centre was constructed on derelict land and has an eye-catching appearance. Since its opening, it has become an important sporting facility and encouraged interest in cycle racing and improved performances by English racing cyclists. (*D. Brearley*)

The granting of the Commonwealth Games to Manchester was the impetus for the construction of a new stadium in the eastern part of the city on former industrial land. At present (2001) the stadium is nearing completion in readiness for the Games in 2002. When the Games have ended, it has been suggested that Manchester City FC will move from Maine Road to the stadium. As well as the stadium and the velodrome, Manchester has been able to build an Olympic-sized swimming pool on Oxford Road for use during the Games. The pool's location close to the universities means that it should be well used not only by those at the universities, but also by the general public as it is within easy reach of the city centre and has good transport links. (*D. Brearley*)

Acknowledgements

Compiling this selection of illustrations to show Manchester past and present has been a challenge in trying to decide which changes to include. To some extent the decision has been made more difficult by the fact that the IRA bomb of 1996 has resulted in two major redevelopments taking place since the end of the Second World War in the cathedral area. With limited space it has only been possible to select some of the changes and to show what was there and what is there now. In some cases the changes are not visible as they have taken place within the building itself. This book concentrates on the centre of Manchester, but this does not mean to say that changes did not take place in the suburbs. There have been many changes here, but to do them full justice they require a book of their own.

I would like to thank all those who have helped in any way whatsoever, either by lending photographs or providing information. In particular, I would like to thank Dr M. Powell of Chetham's Library and George Turnbull of the Greater Manchester Transport Museum for permission to use some of their illustrations. I would also like to thank the staff of Manchester Local Studies Unit for their help and in particular Paula Moorhouse, who organised the copying of the pictures from the Unit's collection. I would also like to thank Sutton Publishing for asking me to compile this book, and all those who have taken and preserved photographs from the past without which such books would not be possible.

Although I have tried to trace the owners of all those illustrations which required permission to reproduce, there are several for which there is no indication of their ownership. I apologise for any infringement of copyright that might have occurred as a result of this failure and hope that the owners will accept this apology.

Special thanks must be given to David Brearley who has made copies of old photographs for this book and taken the new ones for modern Manchester. Without David's help and assistance many of the illustrations in this book could not have been included. I must also thank Peter and Anna for their help and assistance, and finally my wife Hilary, for her help in reading drafts and making suggestions.

Thank you, everyone who has helped. Without you, this book would not have been possible.

AEROFILMS GUIDE

FOOTBALL

GROUNDS

AEROFILMS GUIDE

FOOTBALL
GROUNDS

Edited by Dave Twydell

**DIAL
PRESS**

CONTENTS

Page 1: The old and the new. Millwall's new home is in the foreground while above the Den falls into disrepair.

Page 3: City rivals Liverpool (nearer) and Everton.

First published in 1993 by Dial Press
Reprinted 1993 (Twice)
Second edition 1994

Dial Press is an imprint of Ian Allan Ltd, Terminal House, Station Approach, Shepperton, Surrey KT15 1HY

Printed by Ian Allan Printing Ltd, Coombelands House, Addlestone, Weybridge, Surrey KT15 1HY

Aerial photography ©

 Aerofilms©

Hunting Aerofilms Limited have been specialists in aerial photography since 1919. Their library of aerial photographs, both new and old, is in excess of 1.5 million images. Aerofilms undertake to commission oblique and vertical survey aerial photography which is processed and printed in their specialised photographic laboratory. Digital photomaps are prepared using precision scanners. The Company has been a subsidiary of Hunting plc since 1936.

Free photostatic proofs are available on request for any site held within the collection and price lists will be forwarded detailing the sizes of photographic enlargement available without obigation to purchase.

Text © Ian Allan Ltd 1993, 1994
Football action photography © Empics
Photographs of Wembley reproduced by kind permission of Wembley plc

ISBN 0 7110 2301 8

Editor's Note

The rapid and continuing changes to English Football Grounds provoked the first edition of the *Aerofilms Guide – Football Grounds* in the autumn of 1993. The changes continue unabated, and the great success of the first edition has led to this updated version. A welcome addition to this edition is the coverage of all the Scottish Grounds. All the grounds that were known to have visually changed since the 1992/93 season were photographed during the following season, and building work in progress can be seen in some of the pictures. In some cases this work may have been completed after this book went to the printers and in other cases we show grounds as complete and intact where work will have subsequently begun. Additionally a number of previous vertical views have been repeated for convenience, despite new oblique views which have been included. We will, of course, continue to update the coverage as fully as possible in future editions of this book. It was very gratifying to receive many comments of appreciation, and fortunately only a few advising of minor errors in the first edition, which of course have now been corrected. As before we have made every effort to ensure that all the information given in the entries for various clubs is accurate and complete, but changes being made to the grounds and other factors beyond the publisher's control may introduce errors for which the publishers can admit no consequential responsibility.

We would like to thank all the clubs who took the time and trouble to reply to our requests for information and updates (which once again over 70 clubs in England and Wales did). We would also like to thank the Empics photo agency of Nottingham who supplied the football action pictures of each club which are also featured in this book.

About the Author

Dave Twydell has, for many years, been a Brentford F.C. supporter and also follows non-League football. His first book *Defunct F.C.* (self-published) in 1986 led to his growing interest in the history of the game and the Football Grounds themselves. Six more books and several booklets followed, including *Grounds For A Change* (the histories of the former Grounds of the Football League Clubs). Formerly a Chartered Structural Engineer, redundancy in 1991 led to the full-time publishing of football books – generally of an historical nature under the 'Yore Publications' banner, with the current assistance of wife (Fay), married daughter (Kara) and hindrance of three-year old grandson (Arran)! Dave is now also a partner in Trans Video Productions, who have included the production of several football videos, notably *English Football Grounds – From Newcastle to Wembley*, for Ian Allan SBS Videos.

WEMBLEY

Wembley Stadium, Wembley HA9 0DW

Telephone: 081-902 8833
Advance Tickets Tel No: 081-900 1234
Brief History: Inaugurated for F.A. Cup Final of 1923, venue for many major national and international matches including World Cup Final of 1966. Also used for major occasions in other sports and as venues for rock concerts and other entertainments.

(Total) Current Capacity: 79,000 (All seated)
Nearest Railway Station: Wembley Complex (BR), Wembley Central (BR & Tube), Wembley Park (tube)
Parking (Car): Limited parking at ground and nearby
Parking (Coach/Bus): As advised by police
Police Force: Metropolitan

ARSENAL

Arsenal Stadium, Avenell Road, Highbury, London, N5 1BU

Telephone: 071 226 0304
Advance Tickets Telephone: 071 359 0131
League: F.A. Premier
Brief History: Founded 1886 as Royal Arsenal, changed to Woolwich Arsenal in 1891, and Arsenal in 1914. Former grounds: Plumstead Common, Sportsman Ground, Manor Ground (twice), moved to Arsenal Stadium (Highbury) in 1913. Record attendance 73,295
(Total) Current Capacity: 38,000 (All seated)

Club Colours: Red shirts with white sleeves, white shorts
Nearest Railway Station: Drayton Park & Finsbury Park. Arsenal (tube)
Parking (Car): Street Parking
Parking (Coach/Bus): Drayton Park
Police Force and Tel No: Metropolitan (071 263 9090)
Disabled Visitors' Facilities
  Wheelchairs: Lower tier East Stand (few)
  Blind: Commentary available

KEY
C Club Offices
E Entrance(s) for visiting supporters

↑ North direction (approx)

❶ Avenell Road
❷ Highbury Hill
❸ Gillespie Road
❹ To Drayton Park BR Station (¼ mile)
❺ Arsenal Tube Station
❻ Clock End

Left: Arsenal's Paul Merson in full flight, leaving Villa's bemused defender Paul McGrath on the deck.

ASTON VILLA

Villa Park, Trinity Road, Birmingham, B6 6HE

Telephone: 021 327 2299
Advance Tickets Telephone: 021 327 5353
Credit Card Sales: 021 327 7373
League: F.A. Premier
Brief History: Founded in 1874. Founder Members Football League (1888). Former Grounds: Aston Park and Lower Aston Grounds & Perry Barr, moved to Villa Park (a development of the Lower Aston Grounds) in 1897. Record attendance 76,588
(Total) Current Capacity: 40,000 All seated (November 1994)
Visiting Supporters Allocation: 4,510 (4,510 Seated)
Club Colours: Claret with blue stripe shirts, white shorts.

Nearest Railway Station: Witton
Parking (Car): Asda car park, Aston Hall Road
Parking (Coach/Bus): Asda car park, Aston Hall Road (special coach park for visiting supporters situated in Witton Lane).
Police Force and Tel No: West Midlands (021) 322 6010
Disabled Visitors' Facilities
 Wheelchairs: Trinity Road Stand section
 Blind: Commentary by arrangement
Anticipated Development(s): Holte End Stand being redeveloped for completion November 1994.

KEY

C Club Offices
S Club Shop
E Entrance(s) for visiting supporters
R Refreshment bars for visiting supporters
T Toilets for visiting supporters

↑ North direction (approx)

❶ B4137 Witton Lane
❷ B4140 Witton Road
❸ Trinity Road
❹ A4040 Aston Lane to A34 Walsall Road
❺ To Aston Expressway & M6
❻ Holte End
❼ Visitors' Car Park

Left: Surely one of the most exciting sights in football, Dalian Atkinson with the ball at his feet against Slovan Bratislava in Sept 1993.

BARNET

Underhill Stadium, Barnet Lane, Barnet, Herts, EN5 2BE

Telephone: 081 441 6932
Advance Tickets Telephone: 081 449 4173
Credit Card Bookings: 081 441 1677
League: 3rd Division
Brief History: Founded 1888 as Barnet Alston. Changed name to Barnet (1919). Former grounds: Queens Road & Totteridge Lane. Promoted to Football League 1991. Record attendance 11,026.
(Total) Current Capacity: 4,072 (1,000 Seated)
Visiting Supporters Allocation: 904 (None Seated)

Club Colours: Amber & Black striped shirts, black shorts.
Nearest Railway Station: New Barnet (High Barnet - Tube)
Parking (Car): Street Parking & High Barnet Station
Parking (Coach/Bus): As directed by Police
Police Force and Tel No: Metropolitan (081) 200 2212
Disabled Visitors' Facilities
  Wheelchairs: Barnet Lane (Social Club end - few spaces)
  Blind: No special facility

KEY

C Club Offices
S Club Shop
E Entrance(s) for visiting supporters
R Refreshment bars for visiting supporters
T Toilets for visiting supporters

↑ North direction (approx)

❶ Barnet Lane
❷ Westcombe Drive
❸ A1000 Barnet Hill
❹ New Barnet BR Station (1 mile)
❺ To High Barnet Tube Station, M1 & M25

Left: PFA Representative and highly experienced Brian Marwood lending his talents to the Bees during their ill-fated introduction to Division Two football.

BARNSLEY

Oakwell Ground, Grove Street, Barnsley, S71 1ET

Tel No: 0226 295353
Advance Tickets Tel No: 0226 295353
League: 1st Division
Brief History: Founded 1887 as Barnsley St Peter's, changed name to Barnsley in 1897. Former Ground: Doncaster Road, Worsboro Bridge until 1888. Record attendance 40,255.
(Total) Current Capacity: 27,398 (9,631 Seated)
Club Colours: Red shirts, white shorts

Nearest Railway Station: Barnsley Exchange
Parking (Car): Queen's Ground car park
Parking (Coach/Bus): Queen's Ground car park
Police Force and Tel No: South Yorkshire (0226) 206161
Disabled Visitors Facilities
    Wheelchairs: Purpose Built Disabled Stand
    Blind: Commentary available

KEY
C Club Offices
S Club Shop
E Entrance(s) for visiting supporters
R Refreshment bars for visiting supporters
T Toilets for visiting supporters

↑ North direction (approx)

❶ A628 Pontefract Road
❷ A61
❸ M1 Junction 37 (2 miles)
❹ Queen's Ground Car Park

Right: Still in a red shirt, but now carrying the badge of Barnsley, Player-manager Viv Anderson now coming to terms with the task.

BIRMINGHAM CITY

St Andrew's, St. Andrew's Street, Birmingham, B9 4NH

Tel No: 021 772 0101
Advance Tickets Tel No: 021 772 0101
League: 2nd Division
Brief History: Founded 1875, as Small Heath
Alliance. Changed to Small Heath in 1888,
Birmingham in 1905, Birmingham City in
1945. Former Grounds: Arthur Street,
Ladypool Road, Muntz Street, moved to St.
Andrew's in 1906. Record attendance 68,844.
(Total) Current Capacity: 27,545 (8,395
Seated)
Visiting Supporters' Allocation: 5,700 (808
Seated)

Club Colours: Blue & white shirts, white shorts
Nearest Railway Station: Birmingham New
Street
Parking (Car): Street parking, plus Coventry
Road & Cattell Road car parks
Parking (Coach/Bus): Tilton Road
Police Force and Tel No: West Midlands (021)
772 1169
Disabled Visitors' Facilities
Wheelchairs: Remploy stand (St. Andrew's
Street), advanced notice required.
Blind: No special facilities.

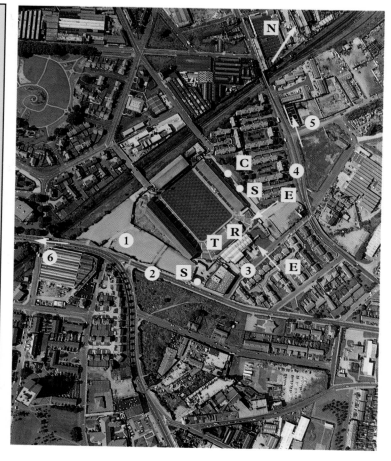

KEY
- **C** Club Offices
- **S** Club Shop
- **E** Entrance(s) for visiting
  supporters
- **R** Refreshment bars for visiting
  supporters
- **T** Toilets for visiting supporters

⬆ North direction (approx)

❶ Car Park
❷ B4128 Cattell Road
❸ Tilton Road
❹ Garrison Lane
❺ To A4540 & A38 (M)
❻ To City Centre and New
Street BR Station (1½ miles)

**Right: Paul Peschisolido –
the subject of much Press
attention and the target of
many top clubs – holds off
the challenge of Wolves'
Rankin.**

BLACKBURN ROVERS

Ewood Park, Blackburn, Lancashire, BB2 4JF

Telephone: 0254 55432
Advance Tickets Tel No: 0254 55432 (696767 Credit card line)
League: F.A. Premier
Brief History: Founded 1875. Former Grounds: Oozebooth, Pleasington Cricket Ground, Alexandra Meadows. Moved to Ewood Park in 1890. Founder members of Football League (1888). Record attendance 61,783.
(Total) Current Capacity: c30,000 All seater
Club Colours: Blue & white halved shirts, white shorts

Nearest Railway Station: Blackburn
Parking (Car): Street parking
Parking (Coach/Bus): As directed by Police
Police Force and Tel No: Lancashire (0254 51212)
Disabled Visitors' Facilities
 Wheelchairs :Walkersteel Stand (Riverside Lane) - few
 Blind: Commentary available
Anticipated Development(s): (Editor's note: Near total redevelopment of ground by end 1994. Update information not advised.)

KEY

↑ North direction (approx)

❶ A666 Great Bolton Street
❷ Nuttall Street
❸ Kidder Street
❹ Town Centre & Blackburn Central BR Station (1½ miles)
❺ To Darwen and Bolton

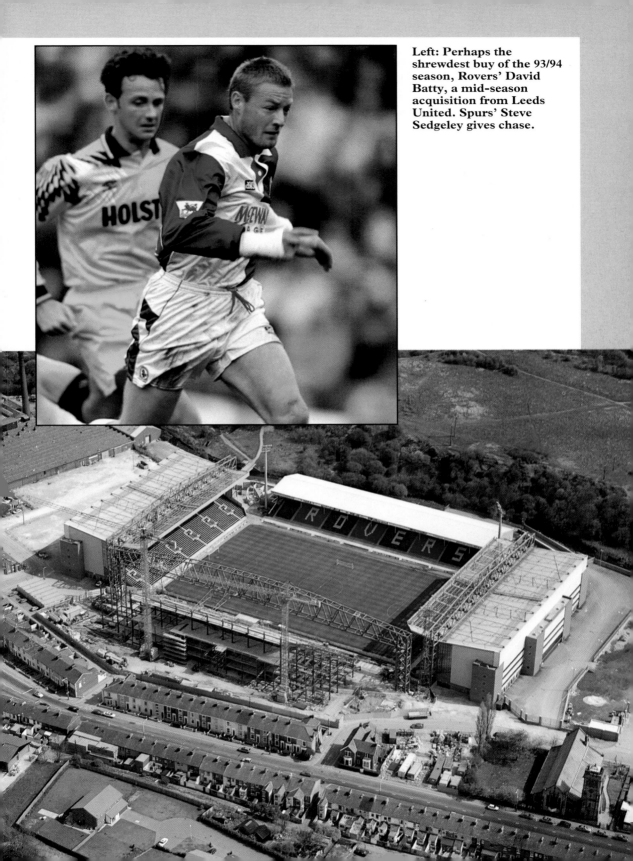

Left: Perhaps the shrewdest buy of the 93/94 season, Rovers' David Batty, a mid-season acquisition from Leeds United. Spurs' Steve Sedgeley gives chase.

BLACKPOOL

Bloomfield Road, Blackpool, Lancashire, FY1 6JJ

Telephone: 0253 404331
Advance Tickets Tel No: 0253 404331
League: 2nd Division
Brief History: Founded 1887, merged with 'South Shore' (1899). Former grounds: Raikes Hall (twice) and Athletic Grounds, Stanley Park. South Shore played at Cow Cap Lane, moved to Bloomfield Road in 1899. Record attendance 38,098
(Total) Current Capacity: 10,337 (2,987 Seated)
Visiting Supporters' Allocation: 2,500 min.(None Seated)
Club Colours: Tangerine shirts, white shorts

Nearest Railway Station: Blackpool South
Parking (Car): At Ground & street parking (also behind West Stand - from M55)
Parking (Coach/Bus): Mecca car park (behind East End, (also behind West Stand - from M55)
Police Force and Tel No: Lancashire (0253 293933)
Disabled Visitors' Facilities
  Wheelchairs: By players entrance
  Blind: Commentary available
Anticipated Development(s): Plans for new ground/complex in same area anticipated for 1995/96 season.

KEY

C Club Offices
E Entrance(s) for visiting supporters
S Club Shop
R Refreshment bars for visiting supporters
T Toilets for visiting supporters

↑ North direction (approx)

❶ Car Parks
❷ To Blackpool South BR Station (½ mile) and M55 Junction 4
❸ Bloomfield Drive
❹ Central Drive
❺ Henry Street
❻ Blackpool Rugby & Greyhound Stadium
❼ Blackpool Tower

Not the Quinn normally making the headlines, but nonetheless an impressive pose from James Quinn in this Division Two fixture at Bloomfield Road.

BOLTON WANDERERS

Burnden Park, Manchester Road, Bolton, BL3 2QR

Telephone: 0204 389200
Advance Tickets Tel No: 0204 21101
League: 1st Division
Brief History: Founded 1874 as Christ Church until 1877. Former Grounds: several very basic fields were used before move to Pikes Lane in 1880, moved to Burnden Park in 1895. Founder-members of Football League (1888). Record attendance 69,912.
(Total) Current Capacity: 20,800 (8,000 Seated)

Club Colours: White shirts, blue shorts
Nearest Railway Station: Bolton Trinity Street
Parking (Car): Rosehill car park, Manchester Road
Parking (Coach/Bus): Rosehill car park, Manchester Road
Police Force and Tel No: Greater Manchester (0204 22466)
Disabled Visitors' Facilities
  Wheelchairs: Manchester Road (few)
  Blind: No special facility

KEY

E Entrance(s) for visiting supporters

R Refreshment bars for visiting supporters

T Toilets for visiting supporters

↑ North direction (approx)

❶ Car Parks
❷ B6536 Manchester Road
❸ A666 St Peter's Way
❹ Bolton Trinity Street BR Station (1/2 mile)
❺ To M61 Junction 3 (3 miles)
❻ Supermarket

Left: After a stunning season – particularly in the F.A.Cup – John McGinlay was rewarded with a Scottish Cap.

A.F.C. BOURNEMOUTH

Dean Court, Bournemouth, Dorset BH7 7AF

Telephone: 0202 395381
Advance Tickets Tel No: 0202 395381
League: 2nd Division
Brief History: Founded 1890 as Boscombe St. John's, changed to Boscombe (1899), Bournemouth & Boscombe Athletic (1923) and A.F.C. Bournemouth (1971). Former grounds: Kings Park (twice) and Castlemain Road, Pokesdown. Moved to Dean Court in 1910. Record attendance 28,799.
(Total) Current Capacity: 11,880 (3,130 Seated)
Visiting Supporters Allocation: 2,190 (190 Seated Family Stand only).

Club Colours: Red with white `V' shirts, black with white piping shorts.
Nearest Railway Station: Bournemouth
Parking (Car): Large car park adjacent ground
Parking (Coach/Bus): Large car park adjacent ground
Police Force and Tel No: Dorset (0202) 552099
Disabled Visitors' Facilities
  Wheelchairs: South Stand (prior arrangement)
  Blind: No special facility

KEY

C Club Offices
S Club Shop
E Entrance(s) for visiting supporters
R Refreshment bars for visiting supporters
T Toilets for visiting supporters

⬆ North direction (approx)

❶ Car Park
❷ A338 Wessex Way
❸ To Bournemouth BR Station (1½ miles)
❹ To A31 & M27

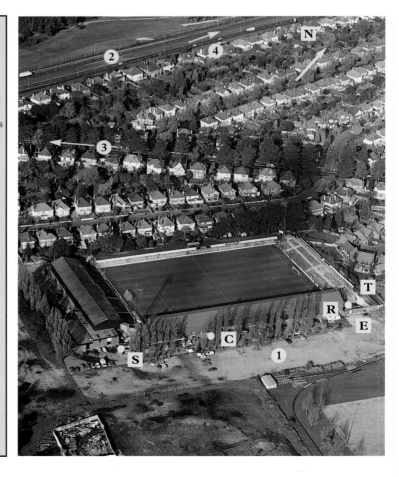

Right: Steve Fletcher of the home team is seen in action against Brighton & Hove Albion in a League Division 2 fixture on 16 October 1993.

BRADFORD CITY

Valley Parade, Bradford, BD8 7DY

Tel No: 0274 306062
Advance Tickets Telephone: 0274 306062
League: 2nd Division
Brief History: Founded 1903 (formerly Manningham Northern Union Rugby Club founded in 1876). Continued use of Valley Parade, joined 2nd Division on re-formation. Record attendance 39,146.
(Total) Current Capacity: 14,810 (6,500 Seated)
Club Colours: Claret & amber shirts, claret shorts

Nearest Railway Station: Bradford Forster Square

Parking (Car): Street parking and car parks

Parking (Coach/Bus): As directed by Police

Police Force and Tel No: West Yorkshire (0274 723422)

Disabled Visitors' Facilities
  Wheelchairs: N & P Stand
  Blind: No special facility

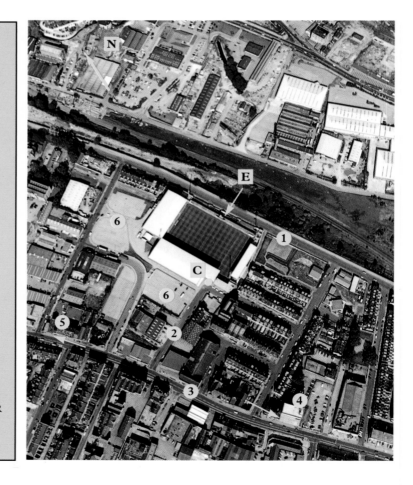

KEY

C Club Offices
E Entrance(s) for visiting supporters

⬆ North direction (approx)

❶ Midland Road
❷ Valley Parade
❸ A650 Manningham Lane
❹ To City Centre, Forster Square and Interchange BR Stations M606 &M62
❺ To Keighley
❻ Car Parks

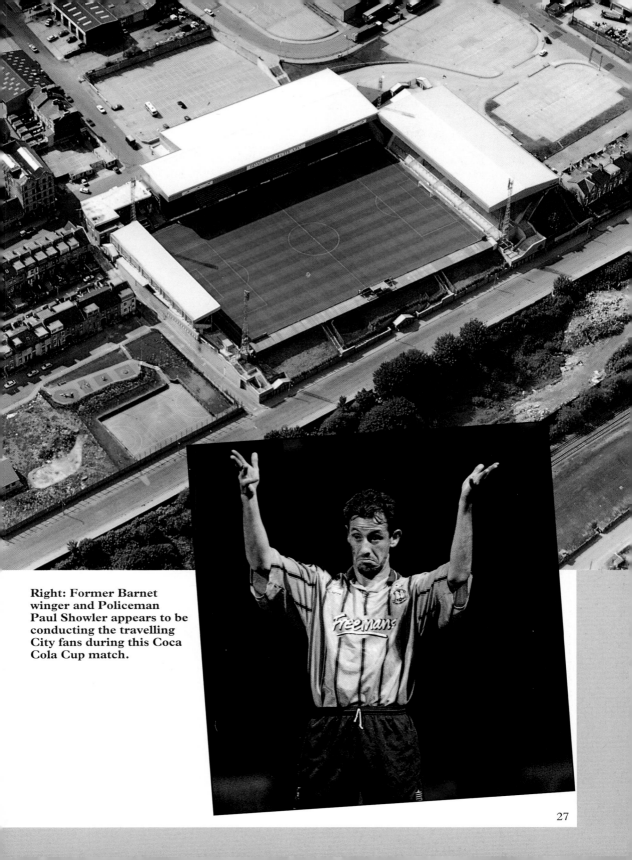

Right: Former Barnet winger and Policeman Paul Showler appears to be conducting the travelling City fans during this Coca Cola Cup match.

BRENTFORD

Griffin Park, Braemar Road, Brentford, Middlesex, TW8 0NT

Tel No: 081 847 2511
Advance Tickets Tel No: 081 847 2511
League: 2nd Division
Brief History: Founded 1889. Former Grounds: Clifden House Ground, Benn's Field (Little Ealing), Shotters Field, Cross Roads, Boston Park Cricket Ground, moved to Griffin Park in 1904. Founder-members Third Division (1920). Record attendance 39,626.
(Total) Current Capacity: 13,870 (4,000 Seated)

Club Colours: Red & white striped shirts, black shorts
Nearest Railway Station: Brentford Central, South Ealing (tube)
Parking (Car): Street parking (restricted)
Parking (Coach/Bus): Layton Road car park
Police Force and Tel No: Metropolitan (081 577 1212)
Disabled Visitors' Facilities
  Wheelchairs: Braemar Road
  Blind: Commentary available

KEY

C Club Offices
S Club Shop
E Entrance(s) for visiting supporters
R Refreshment bars for visiting supporters
T Toilets for visiting supporters

↑ North direction (approx)

❶ Ealing Road
❷ Braemar Road
❸ Brook Road South
❹ To M4 (¼ mile) & South Ealing Tube Station (1 mile)
❺ Brentford Central BR Station
❻ To A315 High Street & Kew Bridge

NEXT TIME... FLY KLM

Left: Shane Westley isn't handling the ball in this League encounter with Burnley, but one could be forgiven for an appeal for a free kick!

29

BRIGHTON & HOVE ALBION

Goldstone Ground, Newtown Road, Hove, Sussex, BN3 7DE

Telephone: 0273 778855
Advance Tickets Telephone: 0273 778855
League: 2nd Division
Brief History: Founded 1900 as Brighton and Hove Rangers, changed to Brighton and Hove Albion in 1902. Former Grounds: Home Farm (Withdean) and County Ground, moved to Goldstone Ground in 1902. Founder members Third Division (1920). Record attendance 36,747.
(Total) Current Capacity: 18,203 (5,274 Seated)
Visiting Supporters Allocation: 3,816 (738 Seated)

Club Colours: Blue & white striped shirts, and matching shorts
Nearest Railway Station: Hove
Parking (Car): Greyhound Stadium and street parking
Parking (Coach/Bus): Conway Street
Police Force and Tel No: Sussex (0273 778922)
Disabled Visitors' Facilities
  Wheelchairs: Newtown Road (South West corner)
  Blind: Commentary available

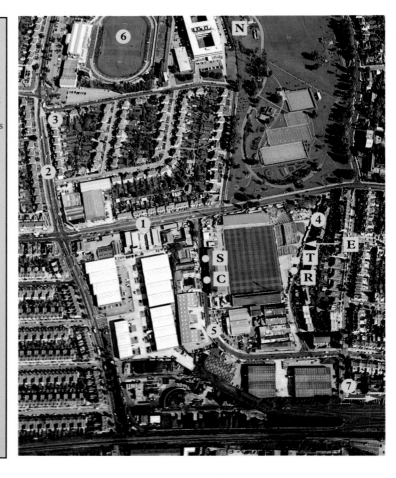

KEY

- **C** Club Offices
- **S** Club Shop
- **E** Entrance(s) for visiting supporters
- **R** Refreshment bars for visiting supporters
- **T** Toilets for visiting supporters

↑ North direction (approx)

- ❶ A27 Old Shoreham Road
- ❷ Nevill Road
- ❸ To A2038 & A23
- ❹ Goldstone Lane
- ❺ Newtown Road
- ❻ Greyhound Stadium
- ❼ Hove BR Station

Left: Steve Foster with familiar headband has now returned to Brighton. It looks as if this honest and reliable defender will finish his League career on the South Coast.

BRISTOL CITY

Ashton Gate, Winterstoke Road, Ashton Road, Bristol, BS3 2EJ

Tel No: 0272 632812
Advance Tickets Tel No: 0272 632812
League: 1st Division
Brief History: Founded 1894 as Bristol South End changed to Bristol City in 1897. Former Ground: St. John's Lane, Bedminster, moved to Ashton Gate in 1904. Record attendance 43,335
(Total) Current Capacity: 23,636 (16,000 Seated)
Club Colours: Red shirts, white shorts

Nearest Railway Station: Bristol Temple Meads
Parking (Car): Street parking
Parking (Coach/Bus): Marsh Road
Police Force and Tel No: Avon/Somerset (0272 277777)
Disabled Visitors' Facilities
   Wheelchairs: Advanced notice required
   Blind: Commentary available
Anticipated Development(s): New stand at open end 1994.

KEY
- **C** Club Offices
- **S** Club Shop
- **E** Entrance(s) for visiting supporters
- **R** Refreshment bars for visiting supporters
- **T** Toilets for visiting supporters

↑ North direction (approx)

- ❶ A370 Ashton Road
- ❷ A3209 Winterstoke Road
- ❸ To Temple Meads Station (1½ miles)
- ❹ To City Centre, A4, M32 & M4
- ❺ Clifton Suspension Bridge
- ❻ River Avon

Left: Junior Bent – one of the fastest forwards in the game – in action during the F.A. Cup replay with Liverpool which City went on to win.

33

BRISTOL ROVERS

Twerton Park, Bath, Avon

(Office: 199, Two Mile Hill Road, Kingswood, Bristol, BS15 1AZ)

Tel No: 0272 352508

Advance Tickets Tel No: 0272 352508

League: 2nd Division

Brief History: Founded 1883 as Black Arabs, changed to Eastville Rovers (1884), Bristol Eastville Rovers (1896) and Bristol Rovers in 1897. Former Grounds: Purdown, Three Acres, The Downs (Horfield), Ridgeway, Bristol Stadium (Eastville) moved to Twerton Park in 1986. Record attendance (at Eastville) 38,472. (At Twerton Park) 9,813.

(Total) Current Capacity: 8,800 (1,006 Seated)

Visiting Supporters' Allocation: 1,125 (None Seated)

Club Colours: Blue & white quartered shirts, white shorts

Nearest Railway Station: Bath Spa

Parking (Car): Street parking (limited)

Parking (Coach/Bus): Avon Street

Police Force and Tel No: Avon/Somerset (0225 444343)

Disabled Visitors Facilities
Wheelchairs: In front of Family stand
Blind: Commentary available by arrangement

Anticipated Development(s): Relocation to New Stadium — 1995/6 season at Severnside, Bristol

---

KEY

E Entrance(s) for visiting supporters

R Refreshment bars for visiting supporters

T Toilets for visiting supporters

↑ North direction (approx)

❶ High Street (Twerton)
❷ A36 Lower Bristol Road
❸ (Bath) City Centre & Bath Spa BR Station (1½ miles)
❹ To Bristol
❺ River Avon

Left: Republic of Ireland International Gary Waddock, now performing consistently in Rovers' colours following his recovery from long term injury.

BURNLEY

Turf Moor, Brunshaw Road, Burnley, Lancs, BB10 4BX

Telephone: 0282 427777
Advance Tickets Telephone: 0282 427777
League: 1st Division
Brief History: Founded 1882, Burnley Rovers (Rugby Club) combined with another Rugby Club, changed to soccer and name to Burnley. Moved from Calder Vale to Turf Moor in 1882. Founder-members Football League (1888). Record attendance 54,775.
(Total) Current Capacity: 22,065 (7,425 Seated)
Club Colours: Claret with blue sleeved shirts, white shorts

Nearest Railway Station: Burnley Central

Parking (Car): Church Street and Fulledge Rec. (car parks)

Parking (Coach/Bus): As directed by Police

Police Force and Tel No: Lancashire (0282 25001)

Disabled Visitors Facilities

Wheelchairs: Endsleigh Stand – Pre-match applications

Blind: Headsets provided with commentary.

KEY

C Club Offices
E Entrance(s) for visiting supporters

↑ North direction (approx)

❶ Brunshaw Road
❷ Belvedere Road
❸ Burnley Central BR Station (1/2 mile)
❹ Cricket Ground

Left: Adrian Heath has found a new lease of life at Turf Moor and has proved an invaluable acquisition for Burnley. Seen here at the match versus Brentford.

BURY

Gigg Lane, Bury, Lancashire, BL9 9HR

Tel No: 061 764 4881
Advance Tickets Tel No: 061 764 4881
League: 3rd Division
Brief History: Founded 1885, no former names or former grounds. Record attendance 35,000
(Total) Current Capacity: 12,900 to be confirmed (Currently 2,000 standing 9,600 Seated)
Club Colours: White shirts, navy shorts

Nearest Railway Station: Bury Interchange
Parking (Car): Street parking
Parking (Coach/Bus): As directed by Police
Police Force and Tel No: Greater Manchester (061 872 5050)
Disabled Visitors Facilities
  Wheelchairs: South Stand
  Blind: Radio commentary (Press box)

KEY

C Club Offices
S Club Shop
E Entrance(s) for visiting supporters
R Refreshment bars for visiting supporters
T Toilets for visiting supporters

↑ North direction (approx)

❶ Car Park
❷ Gigg Lane
❸ A56 Manchester Road
❹ Town Centre & Bury Interchange (Metrolink) (³/₄ mile)

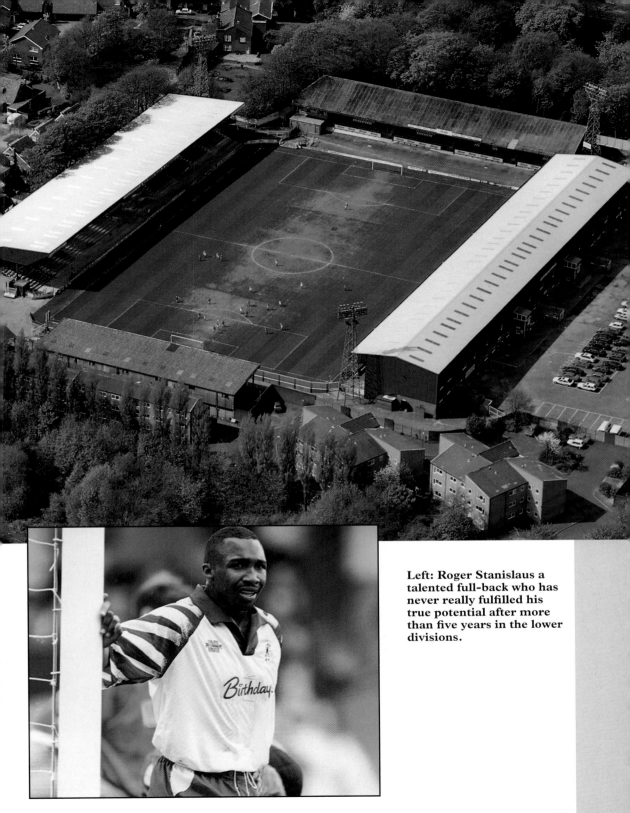

Left: Roger Stanislaus a talented full-back who has never really fulfilled his true potential after more than five years in the lower divisions.

CAMBRIDGE UNITED

Abbey Stadium, Newmarket Road, Cambridge, CB5 8LN

Telephone: 0223 566500
Advance Tickets Telephone: 0223 566500
League: 2nd Division
Brief History: Founded 1913 as Abbey United, changed to Cambridge United in 1949. Former Grounds: Midsummer Common, Stourbridge Common, Station Farm Barnwell (The Celery Trenches) & Parker's Piece, moved to Abbey Stadium in 1933. Record attendance 14,000.
(Total) Current Capacity: 10,100 (3,410 Seated)

Visiting Supporters' Allocation: 2,266 (366 Seated)
Club Colours: Amber shirts, black shorts
Nearest Railway Station: Cambridge (2 miles)
Parking (Car): Coldhams Common
Parking (Coach/Bus): Coldhams Common
Police Force and Tel No: Cambridge (0223 358966)
Disabled Visitors' Facilities
  Wheelchairs: 12 spaces
  Blind: No special facility

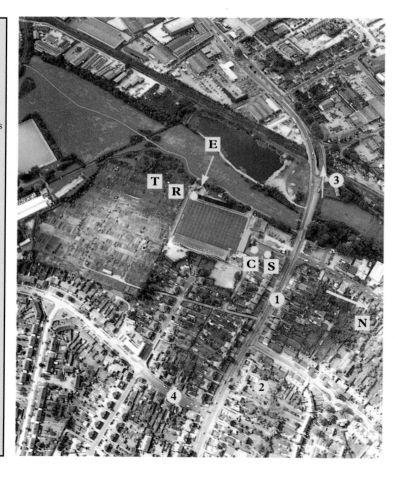

KEY
C Club Offices
S Club Shop
E Entrance(s) for visiting supporters
R Refreshment bars for visiting supporters
T Toilets for visiting supporters

↑ North direction (approx)

❶ A1134 Newmarket Road
❷ To A11 & Newmarket
❸ To City Centre, Cambridge BR Station (2 miles) & M11
❹ Whitehill Road

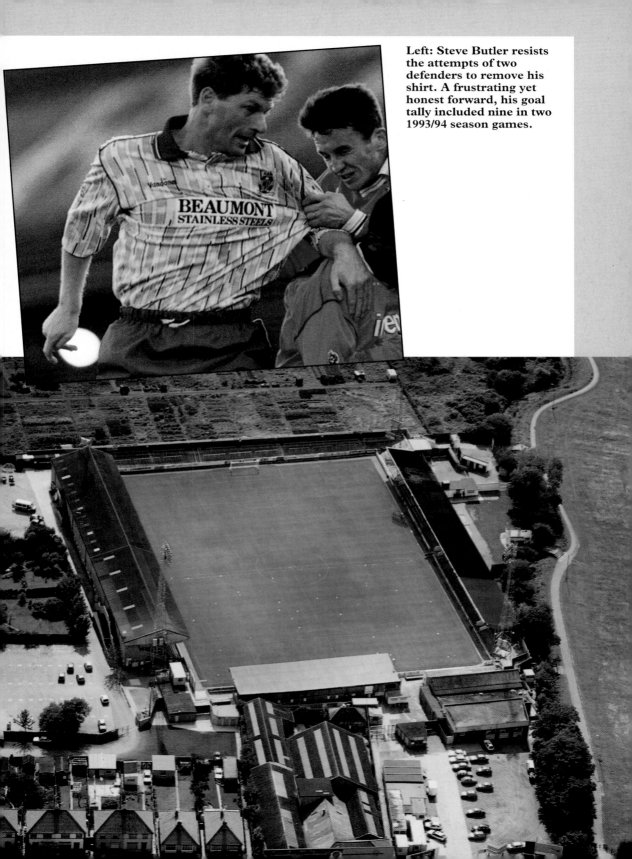

Left: Steve Butler resists the attempts of two defenders to remove his shirt. A frustrating yet honest forward, his goal tally included nine in two 1993/94 season games.

CARDIFF CITY

Ninian Park, Sloper Road, Cardiff, CF1 8SX

Tel No: 0222 398636
Advance Tickets Tel No: 0222 398636
League: 2nd Division
Brief History: Founded 1899. Former Grounds: Riverside Cricket Club, Roath, Sophia Gardens, Cardiff Arms Park & The Harlequins Rugby Ground, moved to Ninian Park in 1910. Ground record attendance 61,566 (Wales v. England, 1961)
(Total) Current Capacity: 20,284 (12,598 Seated)
Club Colours: Blue shirts, blue shorts
Nearest Railway Station: Ninian Park (adjacent) (Cardiff Central 1 mile)

Parking (Car): Opposite Ground, no street parking around ground
Parking (Coach/Bus): Sloper Road
Police Force and Tel No: South Wales (0222 222111)
Disabled Visitors Facilities
  Wheelchairs: Corner Canton Stand/Popular Bank (covered)
  Blind: No special facility
Anticipated Development(s): Popular Bank (AKA 'The Bob Bank') to be converted to all seated in next 1 or 2 years.

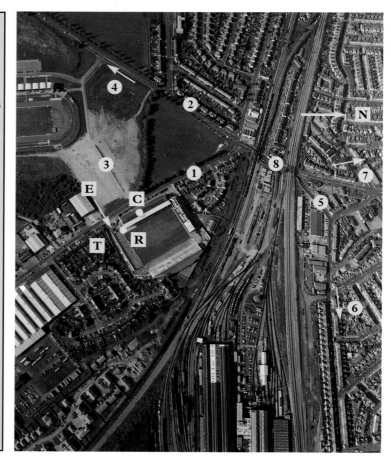

KEY

C Club Offices
E Entrance(s) for visiting supporters
R Refreshment bars for visiting supporters
T Toilets for visiting supporters (Terrace only, when used)

↑ North direction (approx)

❶ Sloper Road
❷ B4267 Leckwith Road
❸ Car Park
❹ To A4232 & M4 Junction 33 (8 miles)
❺ Ninian Park Road
❻ To City Centre & Cardiff Central BR Station (1 mile)
❼ To A48 Western Avenue, A48M, and M4 Junctions 32 and 29
❽ Ninian Park BR station

Left: Much travelled Garry Thompson, signed from Q.P.R. and with over 100 League goals to his credit, in F.A. Cup action against Luton Town.

CARLISLE UNITED

Brunton Park, Warwick Road, Carlisle, CA1 1LL

Tel No: 0228 26237
Advance Tickets Tel No: 0228 26237
League: 3rd Division
Brief History: Founded 1904 as Carlisle United (previously named Shaddongate United). Former Grounds: Millholme Bank and Devonshire Park, moved to Brunton Park in 1909. Record attendance 27,500.
(Total) Current Capacity: 13,913 (2,162 Seated)
Club Colours: Royal blue shirts, white shorts

Nearest Railway Station: Carlisle Citadel
Parking (Car): Rear of ground
Parking (Coach/Bus): St. Aiden's Road car park
Police Force and Tel No: Cumbria (0228 28191)
Disabled Visitors' Facilities
　Wheelchairs: Front of Main Stand (prior arrangement)
　Blind: Commentary available

KEY
- **C** Club Offices
- **E** Entrance(s) for visiting supporters
- **R** Refreshment bars for visiting supporters
- **T** Toilets for visiting supporters

↑ North direction (approx)

❶ A69 Warwick Road
❷ M6 Junction 43
❸ Carlisle Citadel BR Station (1 mile)
❹ Greystone Road
❺ Car Park

Left: Peter Valentine, in action in November 1993, enjoyed a successful season with the Cumbrian team, which culminated in the Third Division play-offs.

CHARLTON ATHLETIC

The Valley, Floyd Road, Charlton, London, SE7 8BL

Tel No: 081 293 4567
Advance Tickets Tel No: 081 293 4567
League: 1st Division
Brief History: Founded 1905. Former grounds: Siemens Meadows, Woolwich Common, Pound Park, Angerstein Athletic Ground, The Mount Catford, Selhurst Park (Crystal Palace FC), Boleyn Ground (West Ham United FC), The Valley (1919-1923, 1924-85, 1992-). Founder Members 3rd Division South. Record attendance 75,031.

(Total) Current Capacity: 14,203 all Seated
Club Colours: Red shirts, white shorts
Nearest Railway Station: Charlton
Parking (Car): Street parking
Parking (Coach/Bus): As directed by Police
Police Force and Tel No: Metropolitan (081 853 8212)
Disabled Visitors Facilities
  Wheelchairs: East/West Stands
  Blind: Commentary, 12 spaces.

KEY

C Club Offices
E Entrance(s) for visiting supporters

⬆ North direction (approx)

❶ Harvey Gardens
❷ A206 Woolwich Road
❸ Valley Grove
❹ Floyd Road
❺ Charlton BR Station
❻ River Thames
❼ Thames Barrier

Left: Cultured full-back Scott Minto enjoys getting the better of Blackburn's David Batty in the F.A. Cup at the Valley.

CHELSEA

Stamford Bridge, Fulham Road, London, SW6 1HS

Tel No: 071 385 5545
Advance Tickets Tel No: 071 385 5545
League: F.A. Premier
Brief History: Founded 1905. Admitted to Football League (2nd Division) on formation. Stamford Bridge venue for F.A. Cup Finals 1919-1922. Record attendance 82,905.
(Total) Current Capacity: 36,000 (19,800 Seated)
Club Colours: Blue shirts, blue shorts
Nearest Railway Station: Fulham Broadway

Parking (Car): Street parking
Parking (Coach/Bus): As directed by Police
Police Force and Tel No: Metropolitan (071 385 1212)
Disabled Visitors' Facilities
  Wheelchairs: East Stand
  Blind: No special facility
Anticipated Development(s): (Editor's note: Update information regarding ground not advised)

KEY

C Club Offices
S Club Shop
E Entrance(s) for visiting supporters
R Refreshment bars for visiting supporters
T Toilets for visiting supporters

↑ North direction (approx)

❶ A308 Fulham Road
❷ Central London
❸ Fulham Broadway Tube Station
❹ South (Shed) Terrace

Left: Mark Stein in close control shortly before his late season injury. Who knows where Chelsea would have finished had he been able to avoid those niggling ailments during 1993/94.

CHESTER CITY

The Deva Stadium, Bumpers Lane, Chester

Tel No: 0244 371376
Advance Tickets Tel No: 0244 373829
League: 2nd Division
Brief History: Founded 1884 from amalgamation of Chester Wanderers and Chester Rovers. Former Grounds: Faulkner Street, Lightfoot Street, Whipcord Lane, Sealand Road, Moss Rose (Macclesfield Town F.C.), moved to Deva Stadium in 1992. Record attendance (Sealand Road) 20,500.
(Total) Current Capacity: 6,000 (3,408 Seated)

Visiting Supporters Allocation: 1,933 max (Seated 637 max.)
Club Colours: Blue/White striped shirts, Black shorts
Nearest Railway Station: Chester (3 miles)
Parking (Car): Car park at ground
Parking (Coach/Bus): Car park at ground
Police Force and Tel No: Cheshire (0244 350222)
Disabled Visitors' Facilities
  Wheelchairs: West and East Stand
  Blind: Facility available

KEY

C Club Offices
S Club Shop
E Entrance(s) for visiting supporters
R Refreshment bars for visiting supporters
T Toilets for visiting supporters

↑ North direction (approx)

❶ Bumpers Lane
❷ To City Centre and Chester BR Station (1½ miles)
❸ Car Park

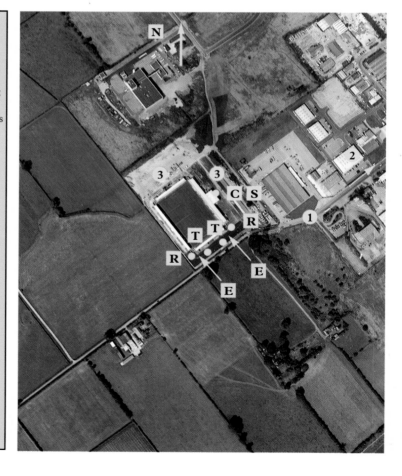

50

Left: Stuart Rimmer taking a breather during a break in the play. A prolific goalscorer in the lower divisions, Rimmer never hit it off on his one sortie to the higher divisions.

CHESTERFIELD

Recreation Ground, Saltergate, Chesterfield, S40 4SX

Tel No: 0246 209765
Advance Tickets Tel No: 0246 209765
League: 3rd Division
Brief History: Founded 1866. Former Ground: Spital Vale. Formerly named Chesterfield Town. Record attendance 30,968
(Total) Current Capacity: 11,308 (2,608 Seated)
Club Colours: Blue and white striped shirts, white shorts
Nearest Railway Station: Chesterfield

Parking (Car): Saltergate car park, street parking
Parking (Coach/Bus): As directed by Police
Police Force and Tel No: Derbyshire (0246 220100)
Disabled Visitors' Facilities
  Wheelchairs: Saltergate Stand
  Blind: No special facility
Anticipated Development(s): (Editor's note: Updated information regarding ground not advised)

KEY	
C	Club Offices
S	Club Shop
E	Entrance(s) for visiting supporters
R	Refreshment bars for visiting supporters
T	Toilets for visiting supporters

↑ North direction (approx)

❶ Saltergate
❷ Cross Street
❸ St Margaret's Drive
❹ A632 West Bars
❺ To A617 & M1 Junction 29

Left: Vastly experienced Trevor Hebberd in typically forceful action during the autumn of 1993, helping the Saltergate side to re-establish itself as more than also-rans in Division Three.

COLCHESTER UNITED

Layer Road Ground, Colchester, CO2 7JJ

Tel No: 0206 574042
Advance Tickets Tel No: 0206 574042
League: 3rd Division
Brief History: Founded 1937, joined Football League 1950, relegated 1990, promoted 1992. Record attendance 19,072.
(Total) Current Capacity: 7,944 (1,150 Seated)
Club Colours: Royal Blue shirts, White shorts

Nearest Railway Station: Colchester Town
Parking (Car): Street parking
Parking (Coach/Bus): Boadicea Way
Police Force and Tel No: Essex (0206 762212)
Disabled Visitors Facilities
    Wheelchairs: Space for six in front of terrace (next to Main Stand)
    Blind: Space for 3 blind persons and 3 guiders.

KEY	
C	Club Offices
S	Club Shop
E	Entrance(s) for visiting supporters
R	Refreshment bars for visiting supporters
T	Toilets for visiting supporters
↑	North direction (approx)
❶	B1026 Layer Road
❷	Town Centre & Colchester Town BR Station (2 miles)
❸	Main Stand
❹	Popular Side

54

Left: United Player-Manager Roy McDonough, probably nearing the end of his playing days, but nonetheless, a vital factor in the Club's successful re-entry to, and re-establishment within, League football.

COVENTRY CITY

Highfield Stadium, King Richard Street, Coventry CV2 4FW.

Tel No: 0203 223535

Advance Tickets Tel No: 0203 225545

League: F.A. Premier

Brief History: Founded 1883 as Singers F.C., changed name to Coventry City in 1898. Former grounds; Dowell's Field, Stoke Road Ground, moved to Highfield Road in 1899. Record attendance, 51,455.

(Total) Current Capacity: 22,600 all seated

Visiting Supporters Allocation: 4,082 all seated

Club Colours: Sky blue shirts, sky blue shorts.

Nearest Railway Station: Coventry.

Parking (Car): Street parking

Parking (Coach/Bus): Gosford Green Coach Park.

Police Force and Tel No: West Midlands (0203 539010)

Disabled Visitors Facilities

  Wheelchairs: Clock Stand (Plus future-section of the East Stand)

  Blind: Clock Stand (booking necessary)

Anticipated Development(s): New East Stand opening 1994/95 season.

KEY

C Club Offices

S Club Shop

E Entrance(s) for visiting supporters

R Refreshment bars for visiting supporters

T Toilets for visiting supporters

↑ North direction (approx)

❶ Swan Lane

❷ A4600 Walsgrave Road

❸ Thackhall Street

❹ Coventry BR Station (1 mile)

❺ To M6 Junction 2 and M69

❻ To M45 Junction 1

❼ Gosford Green Coach Park

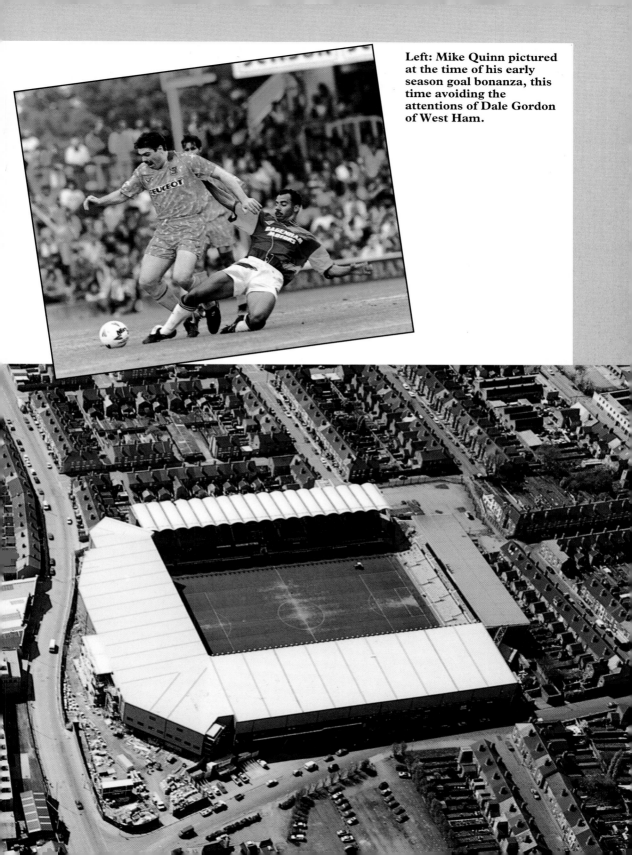

Left: Mike Quinn pictured at the time of his early season goal bonanza, this time avoiding the attentions of Dale Gordon of West Ham.

CREWE ALEXANDRA

Gresty Road Ground, Crewe, Cheshire, CW2 6EB

Tel No: 0270 213014
Advance Tickets Tel No: 0270 213014
League: 2nd Division
Brief History: Founded 1877. Former Grounds; Alexandra Recreation ground (Nantwich Road), Earle Street Cricket Ground, Edleston Road, Old Sheds Fields, Gresty Road (Adjacent to current Ground), moved to current Ground in 1906. Founder members of 2nd Division (1892) until 1896. Founder members of 3rd Division North (1921). Record attendance 20,000.
(Total) Current Capacity: 7,200 (1,200 Seated)

Visiting Supporters' Allocation: 1,500
Club Colours: Red Shirts, White Shorts.
Nearest Railway Station: Crewe.
Parking (Car): Car Park at Ground
Parking (Coach/Bus): Car Park at Ground
Police Force and Tel No: Cheshire (0270 500222)
Disabled Visitors' Facilities
  Wheelchairs: Corner Popular Stand/Family area
  Blind: Commentary available

KEY
- **C** Club Offices
- **S** Club Shop
- **E** Entrance(s) for visiting supporters
- **R** Refreshment bars for visiting supporters
- **T** Toilets for visiting supporters

↑ North direction (approx)

❶ Crewe BR Station
❷ Car Park
❸ Gresty Road
❹ A534 Nantwich Road
❺ A5020 to M6 Junction 16
❻ To M6 Junction 17

Left: Another successful season for 'Alex' culminating in automatic promotion to Division Two. Stuart Evans has seen it all before and was an important factor in the achievement of this promotion.

CRYSTAL PALACE

Selhurst Park, London, SE25 6PU

Tel No: 081 653 1000
Advance Tickets Tel No: 081 771 8841
League: FA Premier
Brief History: Founded 1905. Former Grounds: The Crystal Palace (F.A. Cup Finals venue), London County Athletic Ground (Herne Hill), The Nest (Croydon Common Athletic Ground), moved to Selhurst Park in 1924. Founder members 3rd Division (1920). Record attendance 51,482.
(Total) Current Capacity: 17,619 all seated
Visiting Supporters Allocation: 2,337 all seated

Club Colours: Red with blue striped shirts, red shorts
Nearest Railway Station: Selhurst, Norwood Junction & Thornton Heath
Parking (Car): Street parking & Sainsbury's car park
Parking (Coach/Bus): Thornton Heath
Police Force and Tel No: Metropolitan (081 653 8568)
Disabled Visitors' Facilities
　Wheelchairs: Park Road Stand (limited)
　Blind: Commentary available

KEY

C Club Offices
S Club Shop
E Entrance(s) for visiting supporters
T Toilets for visiting supporters

↑ North direction (approx)

❶ Whitehorse Lane
❷ Park Road
❸ A213 Selhurst Road
❹ Selhurst BR Station (1/2 mile)
❺ Norwood Junction BR Station
❻ Thornton Heath BR Station (1/2 mile)
❼ Car Park (Sainsbury's)

Left: The predatory Chris Armstrong is sure to cause a few headaches in the top flight and an England cap may not be far away.

DARLINGTON

Feethams Ground, Darlington, DL1 5JB

Tel No: 0325 465097
Advance Tickets Tel No: 0325 465097
League: 3rd Division
Brief History: Founded 1883. Founder Members of 3rd Division North (1921), Relegated from 4th Division (1989). Promoted from GM Vauxhall Conference in 1990. Record attendance 21,023.
(Total) Current Capacity: 9,957 (1,120 Seated)
Visiting Supporters' Allocation: 1,200 (250 Seated)

Club Colours: White and Black Shirts, Black Shorts.
Nearest Railway Station: Darlington
Parking (Car): Street parking
Parking (Coach/Bus): As directed by Police
Police Force and Tel No: Durham (0325 467681)
Disabled Visitors' Facilities
   Wheelchairs: East Stand
   Blind: No special facility

KEY

C Club Offices
S Club Shop
E Entrance(s) for visiting supporters
R Refreshment bars for visiting supporters
T Toilets for visiting supporters

↑ North direction (approx)

❶ Polam Lane
❷ Victoria Embankment
❸ Feethams Cricket Ground
❹ Victoria Road
❺ Darlington BR Station (¼ mile)
❻ To A1 (M)

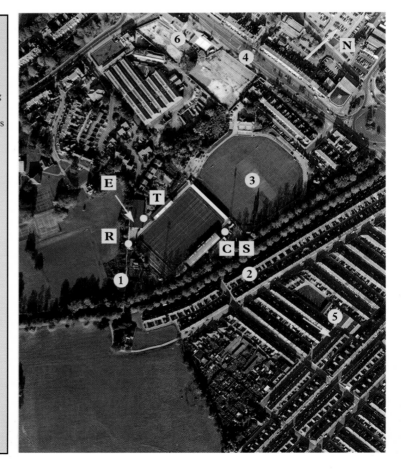

Left: Darlington's Steven Ball (on the right) is having a few problems with the challenge of Kevin Summerfield of Champions to be Shrewsbury Town.

DERBY COUNTY

Baseball Ground, Shaftesbury Crescent, Derby, DE3 8NB

Tel No: 0332 340105
Advance Tickets Telephone: 0332 340105
League: 1st Division
Brief History: Founded 1884. Former Ground: The Racecourse Ground, moved to Baseball Ground in 1894. Founder-members of the Football League (1888). Record attendance 41,826.
(Total) Current Capacity: 19,500 (14,800 Seated)

Club Colours: White shirts, black shorts
Nearest Railway Station: Derby Midland and Ramsline Halt (specials)
Parking (Car): Several car parks
Parking (Coach/Bus): Russel Street
Police Force and Tel No: Derbyshire (0332 290100)
Disabled Visitors' Facilities
    Wheelchairs: Vulcan Street
    Blind: Commentary available

KEY

C Club Offices
S Club Shop
E Entrance(s) for visiting supporters

↑ North direction (approx)

❶ Shaftesbury Crescent
❷ Colombo Street
❸ A514 Osmaston Road
❹ To Derby Midland BR Station (1 mile)
❺ To Ring Road, A6 & M1 Junction 24
❻ Ramsline Halt (BR Specials)

Left: Diminutive Marco Gabiadini, sure to be in the goals wherever he plies his trade, holds off the attentions of Gareth Southgate of Crystal Palace.

DONCASTER ROVERS

Belle Vue, Bawtry Road, Doncaster DN4 5HT

Tel No: 0302 539441
Advance Tickets Tel No: 0302 539441
League: 3rd Division
Brief History: Founded 1879. Former Grounds: Town Moor, Belle Vue (not current Ground), Deaf School Playing Field (later name Intake Ground), Bennetthorpe, moved to Belle Vue (former name Low Pasture) in 1922. Record attendance 37,099.
(Total) Current Capacity: 6,535 (1,259 Seated)

Club Colours: White with Red trim Shirts, White Shorts.
Nearest Railway Station: Doncaster
Parking (Car): Car Park at ground
Parking (Coach/Bus): Car Park at ground
Police Force and Tel No: South Yorkshire (0302 366744)
Disabled Visitors' Facilities
　Wheelchairs: Bawtry Road
　Blind: No special facility

KEY
- **C** Club Offices
- **S** Club Shop
- **E** Entrance(s) for visiting supporters
- **R** Refreshment bars for visiting supporters
- **T** Toilets for visiting supporters

↑ North direction (approx)

❶ A638 Bawtry Road
❷ Racecourse
❸ Car Park
❹ To Doncaster BR Station & A1(M) (3 miles)
❺ To A630 & M18 Junction 4

Left: Don Page in 'Donny' away colours. Not too long ago, Page was a sought after forward whilst at Wigan but big money interest seems to have waned.

EVERTON

Goodison Park, Goodison Road, Liverpool, L4 4EL

Tel No: 051 521 2020
Advance Tickets Telephone: 051 521 2020
Dial a Seat: 051 525 1231
League: FA Premier
Brief History: Founded 1879 as St. Domingo, changed to Everton in 1880. Former Grounds: Stanley Park, Priory Road and Anfield (Liverpool F.C. Ground), moved to Goodison Park in 1892. Founder-members Football League (1888). Record attendance 78,229.
(Total) Current Capacity: 40,000 all seated

Club Colours: Blue shirts, white shorts
Nearest Railway Station: Liverpool Lime Street
Parking (Car): Corner of Utting & Priory Avenues
Parking (Coach/Bus): Priory Road
Police Force and Tel No: Merseyside (051 709 6010)
Disabled Visitors Facilities
   Wheelchairs: Park End Stand.
   Blind: Commentary available

KEY

C Club Offices
S Club Shop
E Entrance(s) for visiting supporters
R Refreshment bars for visiting supporters
T Toilets for visiting supporters

↑ North direction (approx)

❶ A580 Walton Road
❷ Bullens Road
❸ Goodison Road
❹ Car Park
❺ Liverpool Lime Street BR Station (2 miles)
❻ To M57 Junction 2, 4 and 5
❼ Stanley Park

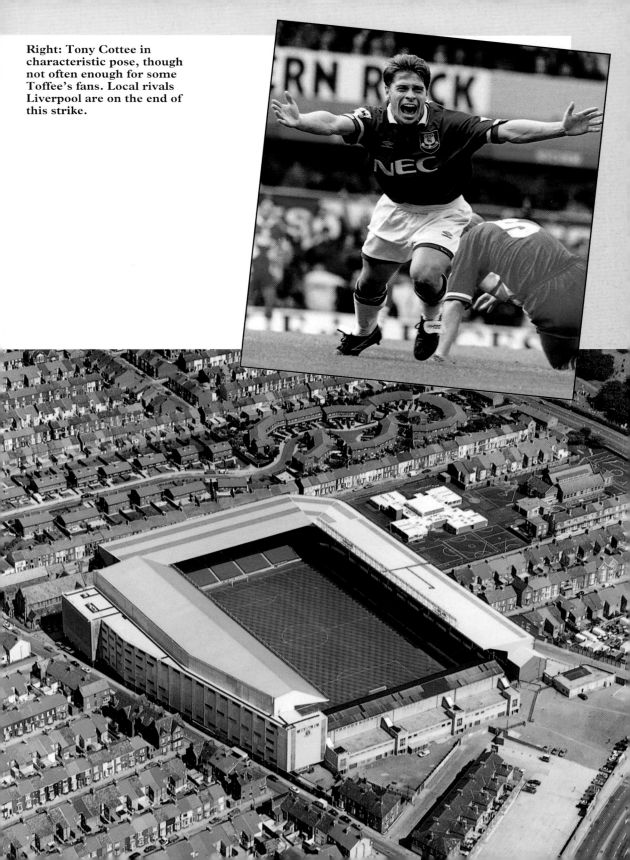

Right: Tony Cottee in characteristic pose, though not often enough for some Toffee's fans. Local rivals Liverpool are on the end of this strike.

EXETER CITY

St. James Park, Exeter, EX4 6PX

Tel No: 0392 54073
Advance Tickets Tel No: 0392 54073
League: 3rd Division
Brief History: Founded in 1904. (From amalgamation of St. Sidwell United and Exeter United.) Founder-members Third Division (1920). Record attendance 20,984.
(Total) Current Capacity: 10,570 (1,608 Seated)
Club Colours: Red and white striped shirts, white shorts

Nearest Railway Station: Exeter St. James Park
Parking (Car): National Car Park and Council Car Parks (No street parking)
Parking (Coach/Bus): Paris Street bus station
Police Force and Tel No: Devon and Cornwall (0392 52101)
Disabled Visitors Facilities
  Wheelchairs: St. James Road entrance (prior booking)
  Blind: No special facility

KEY

C Club Offices
S Club Shop
E Entrance(s) for visiting supporters
T Toilets for visiting supporters

⬆ North direction (approx)

❶ Exeter St. James Park BR Station
❷ St. James Road
❸ Old Tiverton Road
❹ Blackboy Road

70

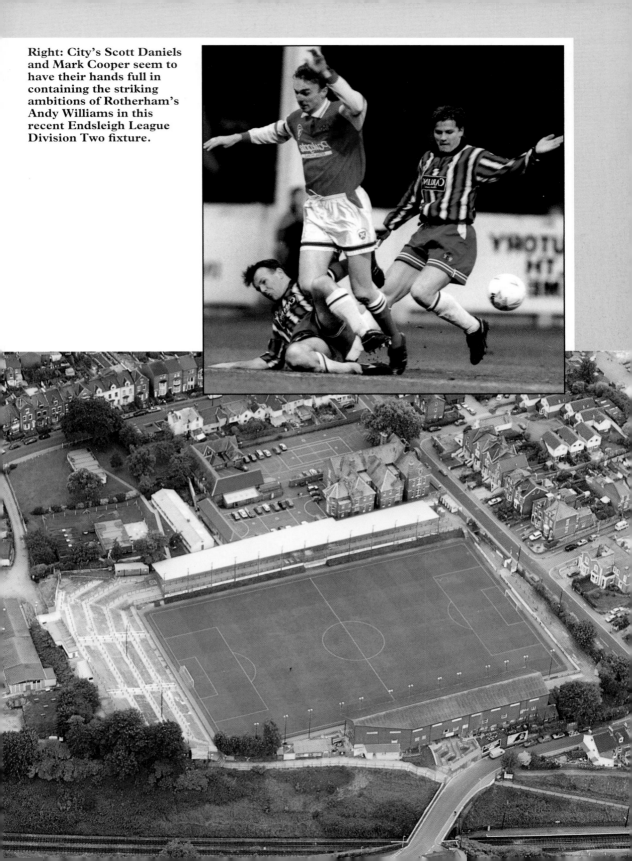

Right: City's Scott Daniels and Mark Cooper seem to have their hands full in containing the striking ambitions of Rotherham's Andy Williams in this recent Endsleigh League Division Two fixture.

FULHAM

Craven Cottage, Stevenage Road, Fulham, London, SW6 6HH

Tel No: 071 736 6561

Advance Tickets Tel No: 071 736 6561

League: 3rd Division

Brief History: Founded in 1879 as St. Andrews Fulham, changed name to Fulham in 1898. Former Grounds: Star Road, Ranelagh Club, Lillie Road, Eel Brook Common, Purser's Cross, Barn Elms and Half Moon (Wasps Rugby Football Ground), moved to Craven Cottage in 1894. Record attendance 49,335.

(Total) Current Capacity: 14,542 (4,652 Seated)

Club Colours: White shirts, black shorts

Nearest Railway Station: Putney Bridge (Tube)

Parking (Car): Street parking

Parking (Coach/Bus): Stevenage Road

Police Force and Tel No: Metropolitan (071 741 6212)

Disabled Visitors' Facilities

Wheelchairs: Miller Stand

Blind: Commentary available (prior arrangement)

KEY

C Club Offices (The Cottage)

S Club Shop

E Entrance(s) for visiting supporters

R Refreshment bars for visiting supporters

T Toilets for visiting supporters

↑ North direction (approx)

❶ River Thames

❷ Stevenage Road

❸ Finlay Street

❹ Putney Bridge Tube Station (1/2 mile)

72

Left: Fulham custodian Jim Stannard, a favourite for many years at Craven Cottage. Prone to awful blunders yet also capable of miraculous saves.

GILLINGHAM

Priestfield Stadium, Redfern Avenue, Gillingham, Kent, ME7 4DD

Tel No: 0634 851854
Advance Tickets Tel No: 0634 576828
League: 3rd Division
Brief History: Founded 1893, as New Brompton, changed name to Gillingham in 1913. Founder-members Third Division (1920). Lost Football League status (1938), re-elected to Third Division South (1950). Record attendance 23,002.
(Total) Current Capacity: 10,422 (1,225 Seated)

Club Colours: Blue shirts, white shorts
Nearest Railway Station: Gillingham
Parking (Car): Street parking
Parking (Coach/Bus): As directed by Police
Police Force and Tel No: Kent (0634 834488)
Disabled Visitors' Facilities
  Wheelchairs: Redfern Avenue
  Blind: No special facility

KEY

C Club Offices
S Club Shop
E Entrance(s) for visiting supporters
R Refreshment bars for visiting supporters
T Toilets for visiting supporters

↑ North direction (approx)

❶ Redfern Avenue
❷ Toronto Road
❸ Gordon Road
❹ Gillingham BR Station (1/4 mile)
❺ Woodlands Road

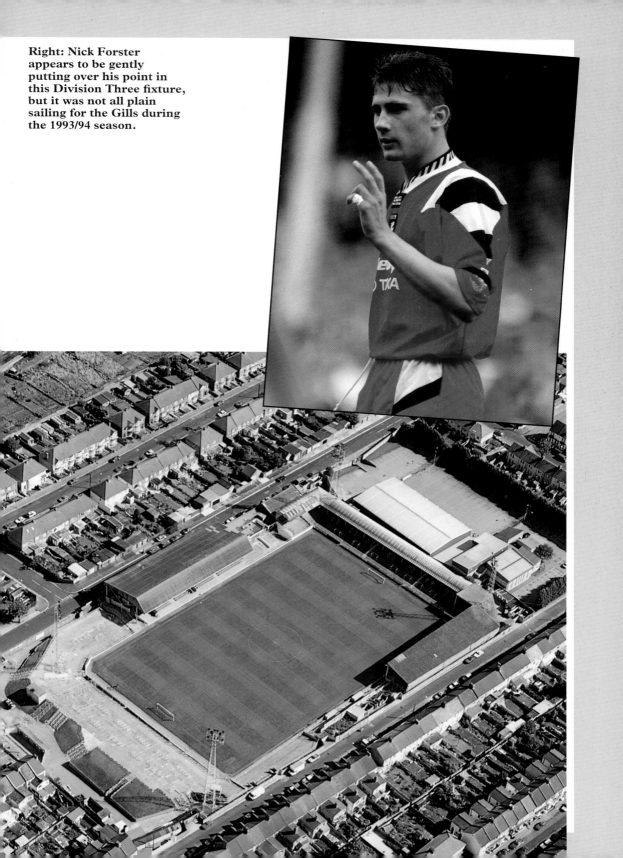

Right: Nick Forster appears to be gently putting over his point in this Division Three fixture, but it was not all plain sailing for the Gills during the 1993/94 season.

GRIMSBY TOWN

Blundell Park, Cleethorpes, DN35 7PY

Tel No: 0472 697111
Advance Tickets Tel No: 0472 697111
League: 1st Division
Brief History: Founded 1878, as Grimsby Pelham, changed name to Grimsby Town in 1879. Former Grounds: Clee Park (two adjacent fields) & Abbey Park, moved to Blundell Park in 1899. Founder-members 2nd Division (1892). Record attendance 31,651.
(Total) Current Capacity: 16,116 (1993/94 season)

Club Colours: Black & white striped shirts, black shorts
Nearest Railway Station: Cleethorpes & New Clee (specials)
Parking (Car): Street Parking
Parking (Coach/Bus): Harrington Street
Police Force and Tel No: Humberside (0472 359171)
Disabled Visitors' Facilities
  Wheelchairs: Harrington Street
  Blind: Commentary available

KEY

C Club Offices (Findus Stand)
S Club Shop
E Entrance(s) for visiting supporters
R Refreshment bars for visiting supporters
T Toilets for visiting supporters

↑ North direction (approx)

❶ A180 Grimsby Road
❷ Cleethorpes BR Station (1½ miles)
❸ To Grimsby and M180 Junction 5
❹ Harrington Street
❺ Constitutional Avenue
❻ Humber Estuary

Left: Former Walsall favourite Craig Shakespeare, now seemingly settled and enjoying life at Blundell Park.

HARTLEPOOL UNITED

Victoria Ground, Clarence Road, Hartlepool, TS24 8BZ

Tel No: 0429 272584
Advance Tickets Tel No: 0429 222077
League: 3rd Division
Brief History: Founded 1908 as Hartlepools United, changed to Hartlepool (1968) and to Hartlepool United in 1977. Founder-members 3rd Division (1921). Record attendance 17,426.
(Total) Current Capacity: 6,721 (2,316 Seated)
Visiting Supporters' Allocation: 680 (Allocation can be extended to 2,070)

Club Colours: Sky and navy blue shirts, navy blue shorts.
Nearest Railway Station: Hartlepool Church Street
Parking (Car): Street parking and rear of clock garage
Parking (Coach/Bus): United bus station
Police Force and Tel No: Cleveland (0429 221151)
Disabled Visitors' Facilities
  Wheelchairs: Raby Road
  Blind: Commentary available

KEY
C Club Offices
S Club Shop
E Entrance(s) for visiting supporters

↑ North direction (approx)

❶ A1088 Clarence Road
❷ Hartlepool Church Street BR Station
❸ A179 Raby Road
❹ Greyhound Stadium
❺ To Middlesbrough A689 & A1(M)

Right: The well-travelled and experienced Keith Houchen is pictured in action for Hartlepool in their game against Wrexham on 20 November 1993.

HEREFORD UNITED

Edgar Street, Hereford, HR4 9JU

Tel No: 0432 276666
Advance Tickets Tel No: 0432 276666
League: 3rd Division
Brief History: Founded 1924, elected to
  Football League 1972. Record attendance
  18,114
(Total) Current Capacity: 13,777 (2,897
  Seated)
Club Colours: White shirts, black shorts

Nearest Railway Station: Hereford
Parking (Car): Merton Meadow & Edgar Street
Parking (Coach/Bus): Cattle Market
Police Force and Tel No: Hereford (0432
  276422)
Disabled Visitors' Facilities
  Wheelchairs: Edgar Street (few)
  Blind: Commentary available

KEY

C Club Offices
S Club Shop
E Entrance(s) for visiting
    supporters
R Refreshment bars for visiting
    supporters
T Toilets for visiting supporters

↑ North direction (approx)

❶ A49 Edgar Street
❷ Blackfriars Street
❸ Hereford BR Station (½ mile)
❹ Newmarket Street
❺ To A438 & M50

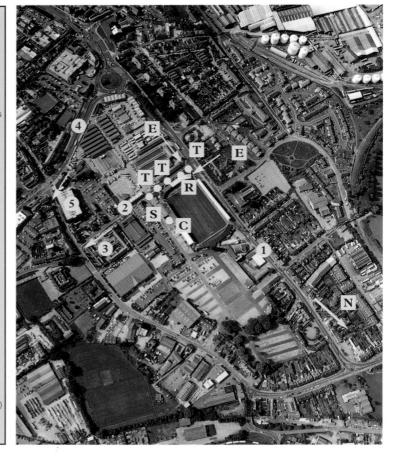

80

Left: Derek Hall scores in the F.A. Cup game versus non-League Bath City and looks suitably impressed. His header from two yards also meets with the approval of his team-mates behind!

HUDDERSFIELD TOWN

Leeds Road, Huddersfield, HD1 6PE

Tel No: 0484 420335
Advance Tickets Tel No: 0484 420335
League: 2nd Division
Brief History: Founded 1908, elected to Football League in 1910. First Club to win the Football League Championship three years in succession. Record attendance 67,037.
(Total) Current Capacity: 17,010 (5,340 Seated)
Visiting Supporters' Allocation: 3,401 (901 Seated)
Club Colours: Blue and white striped shirts, white shorts
Nearest Railway Station: Huddersfield

Parking (Car): Car parks adjacent to ground
Parking (Coach/Bus): Car parks adjacent to ground
Police Force and Tel No: West Yorkshire (0484 422122)
Disabled Visitors' Facilities
  Wheelchairs: Bradley Mills Road (special raised and covered platform).
  Blind: No special facility
Anticipated Development(s): 1994/95 season part occupation, stadium final completion 1995, (Editor's note: Full information regarding new stadium not advised).

KEY

C Club Offices
S Club Shop
E Entrance(s) for visiting supporters
R Refreshment bars for visiting supporters
T Toilets for visiting supporters

↑ North direction (approx)

❶ A62 Leeds Road
❷ Bradley Mills Road
❸ To Leeds and M62 Junction 25
❹ To Huddersfield BR Station (1¼ miles)
❺ Car Parks

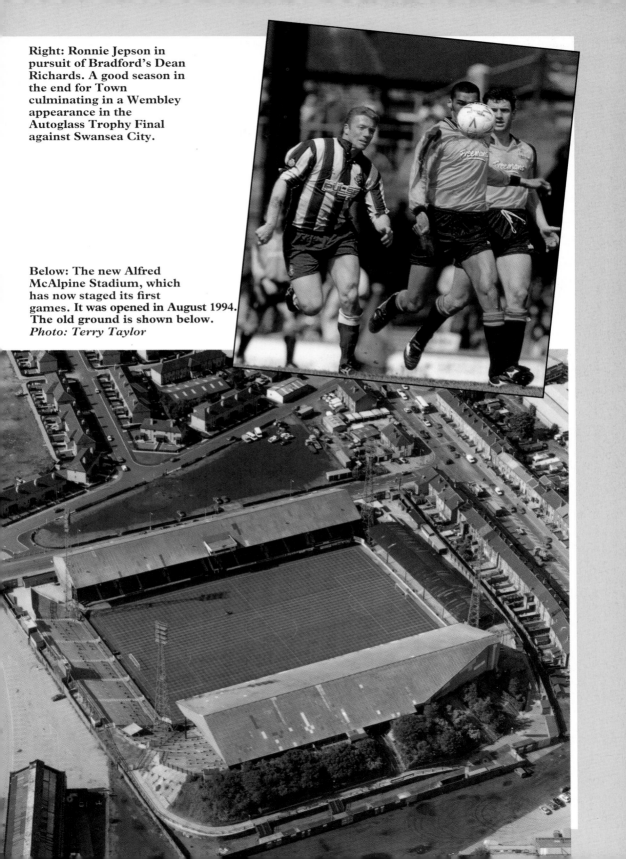

Right: Ronnie Jepson in pursuit of Bradford's Dean Richards. A good season in the end for Town culminating in a Wembley appearance in the Autoglass Trophy Final against Swansea City.

Below: The new Alfred McAlpine Stadium, which has now staged its first games. It was opened in August 1994. The old ground is shown below.
Photo: Terry Taylor

HULL CITY

Boothferry Park, Boothferry Road, Hull, HU4 6EU

Tel No: 0482 51119
Advance Tickets Tel No: 0482 51119
League: 2nd Division
Brief History: Founded 1904. Former grounds: The Boulevard (Hull Rugby League Ground), Dairycoates, Anlaby Road Cricket Circle (Hull Cricket Ground), Anlaby Road, moved to Boothferry Park in 1946. Record attendance 55,019.
(Total) Current Capacity: 16,808 (5,515 Seated)
Visiting Supporters' Allocation: 3,260 (530 Seated)

Club Colours: Amber & black striped shirts, black shorts
Nearest Railway Station: Hull Paragon
Parking (Car): Street Parking and at ground (limited)
Parking (Coach/Bus): At ground
Police Force and Tel No: Humberside (0482 220148)
Disabled Visitors' Facilities
  Wheelchairs: Corner East/South stands
  Blind: Commentary available

KEY

C Club Offices
E Entrance(s) for visiting supporters

↑ North direction (approx)

❶ A63 Boothferry Road
❷ North Road
❸ Hull Paragon BR Station (1½ miles)
❹ To Humber Bridge and M62 Junction 38

Left: City's Graeme Atkinson appears to have run out of puff in his efforts to catch up with this pass in this early 1993/94 season fixture.

IPSWICH TOWN

Portman Road, Ipswich, IP1 2DA

Tel No: 0473 219211

Advance Tickets Tel No: 0473 221133

League: F.A. Premier

Brief History: Founded 1887 as Ipswich Association F.C., changed to Ipswich Town in 1888. Former Grounds: Broom Hill & Brookes Hall, moved to Portman Road in 1888. Record attendance 38,010

(Total) Current Capacity: 22,500 all seated

Visiting Supporters Allocation: 1,500 seated

Club Colours: Blue shirts, white shorts

Nearest Railway Station: Ipswich

Parking (Car): Portman Road, Portman Walk & West End Road

Parking (Coach/Bus): West End Road

Police Force and Tel No: Suffolk (0473 611611)

Disabled Visitors' Facilities
   Wheelchairs: South Stand (Churchmans)
   Blind: Commentary available

KEY

C Club Offices

S Club Shop

E Entrance(s) for visiting supporters

R Refreshment bars for visiting supporters

T Toilets for visiting supporters

⬆ North direction (approx)

❶ A137 West End Road
❷ Portman Walk
❸ Portman Road
❹ Princes Street
❺ Ipswich BR Station
❻ Car Parks

Left: Highly talented Chris Kiwomya performing on the Portman Road stage. Surely a higher stage awaits this crowd pleaser, though Darren Ferguson looks unimpressed.

LEEDS UNITED

Elland Road, Leeds, LS11 0ES

Tel No: 0532 716037

Advance Tickets Tel No: 0532 710710

League: F.A. Premier

Brief History: Founded 1919, formed from the former 'Leeds City' Club, who were disbanded following expulsion from the Football League in October 1919. Joined Football League in 1920. Record attendance 57,892

(Total) Current Capacity: 41,592 (32,392 Seated)

Club Colours: White shirts, white shorts

Nearest Railway Station: Leeds City

Parking (Car): Car parks adjacent to ground

Parking (Coach/Bus): As directed by Police

Police Force and Tel No: West Yorkshire (0532 435353)

Disabled Visitors Facilities

Wheelchairs: West Stand and South Stand

Blind: Commentary available

Anticipated Development(s): New East Stand 17,000 seats, phase one - approx. 5,000 seats — for completion July 1995.

KEY

C Club Offices

S Club Shop

E Entrance(s) for visiting supporters

↑ North direction (approx)

❶ M621

❷ M621 Junction 2

❸ A643 Elland Road

❹ Lowfields Road

❺ To A58

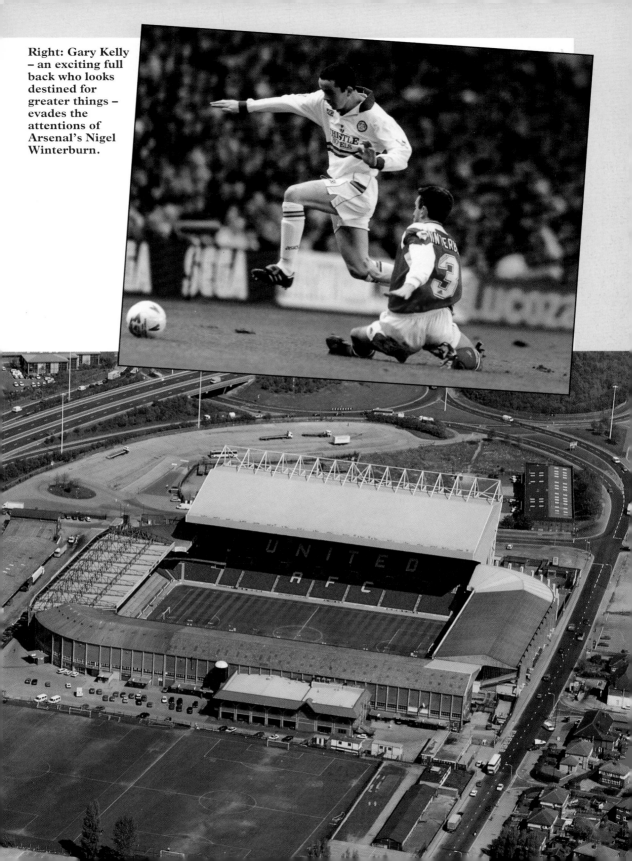

Right: Gary Kelly – an exciting full back who looks destined for greater things – evades the attentions of Arsenal's Nigel Winterburn.

LEICESTER CITY

City Stadium, Filbert Street, Leicester, LE2 7FL

Tel No: 0533 555000
Advance Tickets Tel No: 0533 555000
League: F.A. Premier
Brief History: Founded 1884 as Leicester Fosse, changed name to Leicester City in 1919. Former Grounds: Fosse Road South, Victoria Road, Belgrave Cycle Track, Mill Lane & Aylestone Road Cricket Ground, moved to Filbert Street in 1891. Record attendance 47,298
(Total) Current Capacity: 22,181 (12,833 Seated)

Club Colours: Blue shirts, blue shorts
Nearest Railway Station: Leicester
Parking (Car): NCP car park & street parking
Parking (Coach/Bus): Western Boulevard
Police Force and Tel No: Leicester (0533 530066)

Disabled Visitors' Facilities
   Wheelchairs: Filbert Street
   Blind: No special facility

KEY

C Club Offices
S Club Shop
E Entrance(s) for visiting supporters
R Refreshment bars for visiting supporters
T Toilets for visiting supporters

↑ North direction (approx)

❶ Walnut Street
❷ Filbert Street
❸ Grasmere Street
❹ River Soar
❺ M1 and M69 Junction 21
❻ Leicester BR Station (1 mile)

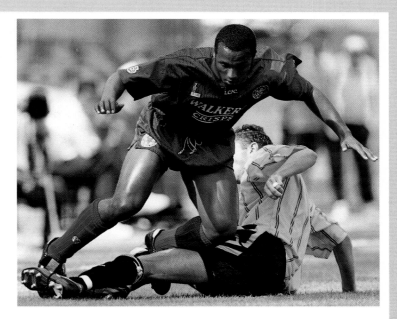

Right: Lightning fast and highly talented, Julian Joachim leaves Millwall's Phil Barber seated on the Filbert Street turf.

LEYTON ORIENT

Leyton Stadium, Brisbane Road, Leyton, London, E10 5NE

Tel No: 081 539 2223
Advance Tickets Tel No: 081 539 2223
League: 2nd Division
Brief History: Founded 1887 as Clapton Orient, from Eagle Cricket Club (formerly Glyn Cricket Club formed in 1881). Changed name to Leyton Orient (1946), Orient (1966), Leyton Orient (1987). Former grounds: Glyn Road, Whittles Athletic Ground, Millfields Road, Lea Bridge Road, Wembley Stadium (2 games), moved to Brisbane Road in 1937. Record attendance 34,345.

(Total) Current Capacity: 18,869 (7,171 Seated)
Club Colours: Red shirts, white shorts
Nearest Railway Station: Leyton (tube), Leyton Midland Road
Parking (Car): Street parking
Parking (Coach/Bus): As directed by Police
Police Force and Tel No: Metropolitan (081 556 8855)
Disabled Visitors Facilities
    Wheelchairs: Windsor Road
    Blind: Match commentary supplied on request

KEY
C Club Offices
S Club Shop
E Entrance(s) for visiting supporters
R Refreshment bars for visiting supporters
T Toilets for visiting supporters

↑ North direction (approx)

❶ Buckingham Road
❷ Oliver Road
❸ A112 High Road Leyton
❹ Leyton Tube Station (¼ mile)
❺ Brisbane Road

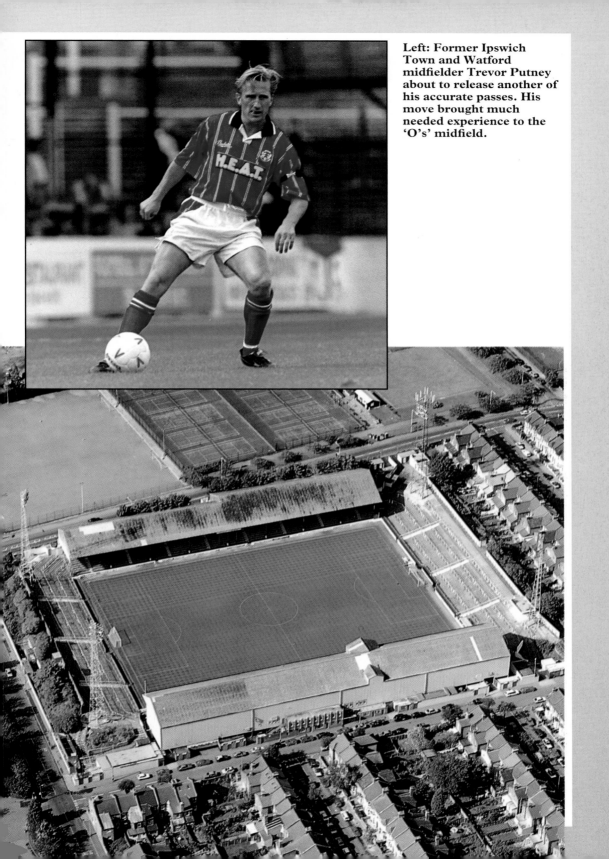

Left: Former Ipswich Town and Watford midfielder Trevor Putney about to release another of his accurate passes. His move brought much needed experience to the 'O's' midfield.

LINCOLN CITY

Sincil Bank, Lincoln, LN5 8LD

Tel No: 0522 522224
Advance Tickets Tel No: 0522 522224
League: 3rd Division
Brief History: Founded 1884. Former Ground: John O'Gaunts Ground, moved to Sincil Bank in 1895. Founder-members 2nd Division Football League (1892). Relegated from 4th Division in 1987, promoted from GM Vauxhall Conference in 1988. Record attendance 23,196.
(Total) Current Capacity: 12,428 (3,271 Seated)
Visiting Supporters' Allocation: 3,716 (641 Seated)

Club Colours: Red & white striped shirts, black shorts
Nearest Railway Station: Lincoln Central
Parking (Car): Adjacent Ground
Parking (Coach/Bus): South Common
Police Force and Tel No: Lincolnshire (0522 529911)
Disabled Visitors' Facilities
  Wheelchairs: South Park Stand
  Blind: No special facility
Anticipated Development(s): Sincil Bank Terrace will be replaced by a new 6,500 all-seater stand. It is anticipated that work will commence in July 1994 and will be completed by January 1995.

KEY
- **C** Club Offices
- **S** Club Shop
- **E** Entrance(s) for visiting supporters
- **R** Refreshment bars for visiting supporters
- **T** Toilets for visiting supporters

↑ North direction (approx)

- ❶ A46 High Street
- ❷ Sincil Bank
- ❸ Sausthorpe Street
- ❹ Cross Street
- ❺ A158 Canwick Road
- ❻ A158 South Park Avenue
- ❼ Car Park
- ❽ Lincoln Central BR Station (1/2 mile)

Left: Much-travelled Nicky Platnauer has tasted life at many big clubs including Coventry City. He now seems to be nearing the end of his playing days, and enjoying himself at Sincel Bank.

LIVERPOOL

Anfield Road, Liverpool, L4 0TH

Tel No: 051 263 2361
Advance Tickets Tel No: 051 260 8680
League: F.A. Premier
Brief History: Founded 1892. Anfield Ground formerly Everton F.C. Ground. Joined Football League in 1893. Record attendance 61,905.
(Total) Current Capacity: 44,431 (27,951 Seated)
Visiting Supporters' Allocation: 3,059 (3,059 Seated)
Club Colours: Red shirts, red shorts
Nearest Railway Station: Kirkdale

Parking (Car): Stanley car park
Parking (Coach/Bus): Priory Road & Pinehurst Avenue
Police Force and Tel No: Merseyside (051 709 6010)
Disabled Visitors' Facilities
  Wheelchairs: Lothair Road
  Blind: Commentary available
Anticipated Development(s): Spion Kop Terrace currently being developed to all-seater with capacity of c10,000.

KEY

C Club Offices
S Club Shop
E Entrance(s) for visiting supporters

↑ North direction (approx)

❶ Car Park
❷ Anfield Road
❸ A5089 Walton Breck Road
❹ Kemlyn Road
❺ Kirkdale BR Station (1 mile)
❻ Utting Avenue
❼ Stanley Park
❽ Spion Kop

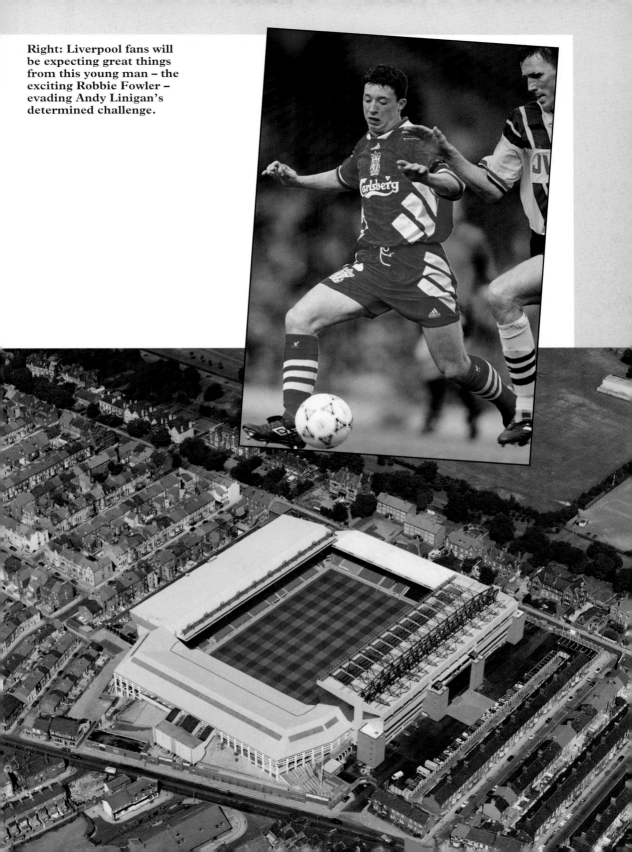

Right: Liverpool fans will be expecting great things from this young man – the exciting Robbie Fowler – evading Andy Linigan's determined challenge.

LUTON TOWN

Kenilworth Road Stadium, 1 Maple Road, Luton, LU4 8AW

Tel No: 0582 411622
Advance Tickets Tel No: 0582 30748
League: 1st Division
Brief History: Founded 1885 from an amalgamation of Wanderers F.C. & Excelsior F.C. Former Grounds: Dallow Lane & Dunstable Road, moved to Kenilworth Road in 1905. Record attendance 30,069.
(Total) Current Capacity: 11,099
Club Colours: White shirts with royal blue & orange stripe on collar & waist. Royal blue shorts with white & orange trim.

Nearest Railway Station: Luton

Parking (Car): Street parking

Parking (Coach/Bus): Luton bus station

Police Force and Tel No: Bedfordshire (0582 401212)

Disabled Visitors' Facilities
 Wheelchairs: Kenilworth Road
 Blind: Commentary available

KEY

C Club Offices
S Club Shop
E Entrance(s) for visiting supporters
R Refreshment bars for visiting supporters
T Toilets for visiting supporters

↑ North direction (approx)

❶ To M1 Junction 11
❷ Wimborne Road
❸ Kenilworth Road
❹ Oak Road
❺ Dunstable Road
❻ Luton BR Station (1 mile)
❼ Ticket Office

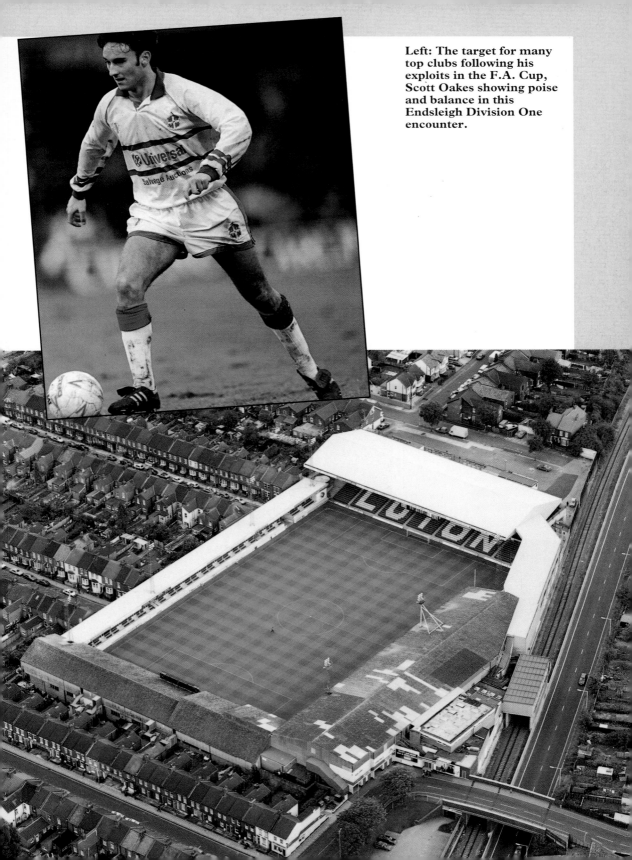

Left: The target for many top clubs following his exploits in the F.A. Cup, Scott Oakes showing poise and balance in this Endsleigh Division One encounter.

MANCHESTER CITY

Maine Road, Moss Side, Manchester, M14 7WN

Tel No: 061 226 1191
Advance Tickets Tel No: 061 226 2224
League: F.A. Premier
Brief History: Founded 1880 as West Gorton, changed name to Ardwick (reformed 1887) and to Manchester City in 1894. Former grounds: Clowes Street, Kirkmanshulme Cricket Club, Donkey Common, Pink Bank Lane & Hyde Road, moved to Maine Road in 1923. Founder-members 2nd Division (1892). Record attendance 84,569 (record for Football League ground).
(Total) Current Capacity: 21,304 (extension applied for)
Visiting Supporters Allocation: None until new Kippax Street Stand is complete, or an extension is granted.

Club Colours: Sky blue shirts, white shorts
Nearest Railway Station: Manchester Piccadilly (2½ miles)
Parking (Car): Street parking & local schools
Parking (Coach/Bus): Kippax Street car park
Police Force and Tel No: Greater Manchester (061 872 5050)
Disabled Visitors' Facilities
   Wheelchairs: Umbro Stand
   Blind: Main Stand 'G' Block
Anticipated Development(s): Seating of Kippax Street Stand during 1994 close season.

KEY

C Club Offices
S Club Shop
E Entrance(s) for visiting supporters

↑ North direction (approx)

❶ Thornton Road
❷ South Upper Lloyd Street
❸ To A5103 Princess Road
❹ To City Centre and Manchester Piccadilly BR Station (2½ miles)
❺ To A6010 & M31 Junction 7
❻ Maine Road

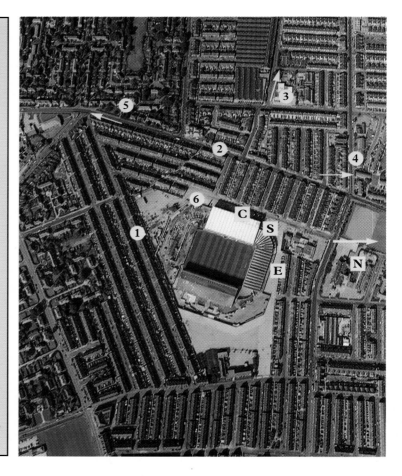

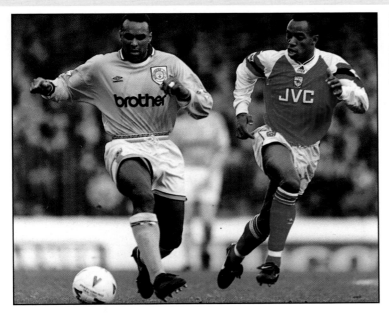

Left: Old pals – City's David Rocastle and Arsenal's Ian Wright pictured in this Premiership encounter at Maine Road.

MANCHESTER UNITED

Old Trafford, Warwick Road North, Manchester, M16 0RA

Tel No: 061 872 1661

Advance Tickets Tel No: 061 872 0199

League: F.A. Premier

Brief History: Founded in 1878 as 'Newton Heath L & Y', later Newton Heath, changed to Manchester United in 1902. Former Grounds: North Road, Monsall & Bank Street, Clayton, moved to Old Trafford in 1910 (used Manchester City F.C. Ground 1941-49). Founder-members Second Division (1892). Record attendance 76,962.

(Total) Current Capacity: 43,500 all seated

Club Colours: Red shirts, white shorts

Nearest Railway Station: At Ground

Parking (Car): Lancashire Cricket Ground & White City

Parking (Coach/Bus): As directed by Police

Police Force and Tel No: Greater Manchester (061 872 5050)

Disabled Visitors' Facilities
  Wheelchairs: In front of Main Stand.
  Blind: Commentary available

KEY

C Club Offices

S Club Shop

↑ North direction (approx)

❶ A5081 Trafford Park Road to M63 Junction 4 (5 miles)
❷ A56 Chester Road
❸ Manchester Ship Canal
❹ Old Trafford Cricket Ground
❺ To Parking and Warwick Road BR Station

Right: A familiar sight for United fans, as Paul Ince assists in the celebration of Ryan Giggs' latest dazzling goal.

MANSFIELD TOWN

Field Mill Ground, Quarry Lane, Mansfield, Notts

Tel No: 0623 23567
Advance Tickets Tel No: 0623 23567
League: 3rd Division
Brief History: Founded 1910 as Mansfield Wesleyans Boys Brigade, changed to Mansfield Town in 1914. Former Grounds: Pelham Street, Newgate Lane & The Prairie, moved to Field Mill in 1919. Record attendance 24,467.
(Total) Current Capacity: 10,315 (3,448 Seated)
Club Colours: Amber with blue trim shirts, Amber shorts with blue trim.

Nearest Railway Station: Mansfield Alfreton Parkway (9 miles)
Parking (Car): Car park at Ground
Parking (Coach/Bus): Car park at Ground
Police Force and Tel No: Nottinghamshire (0623 420999)
Disabled Visitors' Facilities
  Wheelchairs: Bishop Street (Entrance at North end of West stand)
  Blind: No special facility

KEY
C Club Offices
E Entrance(s) for visiting supporters

↑ North direction (approx)

❶ Car Park
❷ Quarry Lane
❸ A60 Nottingham Road to M1 Junction 27
❹ Portland Street
❺ To A38 and M1 Junction 28
❻ Town Centre

Left: A superb action picture of Mansfield's Wayne Fairclough unleashing a shot on the Walsall goal. Evran Wright is the impressed onlooker.

MIDDLESBROUGH

Ayresome Park, Middlesbrough, Cleveland, TS1 4PB

Tel No: 0642 819659
Advance Tickets Tel No: 0642 815996
League: 1st Division
Brief History: Founded 1876. Former Grounds: Archery Ground (Albert Park), Breckon Hill Road, Linthorpe Road, moved to Ayresome Park in 1903. F.A. Amateur Cup winners 1894 & 1897 (joined Football League in 1899). Record attendance 53,596
(Total) Current Capacity: 26,677 (13,146 Seated)
Visiting Supporters' Allocation: 2,342 (502 Seated)

Club Colours: Red shirts with white yoke, white shorts
Nearest Railway Station: Middlesbrough
Parking (Car): Street parking
Parking (Coach/Bus): As directed by Police
Police Force and Tel No: Cleveland (0642 248184)
Disabled Visitors' Facilities
  Wheelchairs: Corner Ayresome Street/Ayresome Park Road
  Blind: Commentary available
Anticipated Development(s): All-seater fully covered new stadium by 1995/96 season.

KEY	
C	Club Offices
S	Club Shop
E	Entrance(s) for visiting supporters
R	Refreshment bars for visiting supporters
T	Toilets for visiting supporters
↑	North direction (approx)
❶	Ayresome Street
❷	Ayresome Park Road
❸	Linthorpe Road
❹	Middlesbrough BR Station (1 mile) and Town Centre

Left: John Hendrie in familiar goalscoring action against Notts County in August 1993. Together with Paul Wilkinson, they have formed a successful striking partnership in Division One.

MILLWALL

New Den, Bolina Road, London, SE16

Tel No: 071 232 1222
Advance Tickets Tel No: 071 231 9999
League: 1st Division
Brief History: Founded 1885 as Millwall Rovers, changed name to Millwall Athletic (1889) and Millwall (1925). Former Grounds: Glengall Road, East Ferry Road (2 separate Grounds), North Greenwich Ground and The Den - Cold Blow Lane - moved to New Den 1993/94 season. Founder-members Third Division (1920). Record attendance (at The Den) 48,672.

(Total) Current Capacity: 20,150 (20,150 Seated)
Club Colours: Blue shirts, Blue shorts
Nearest Railway Station: South Bermondsey or Surrey Docks (tube)
Parking (Car): Juno Way car parking (8 mins. walk)
Parking (Coach/Bus): At Ground
Police Force and Tel No: Metropolitan (071 679 9217)
Disabled Visitors Facilities
   Wheelchairs: Area allocated
   Blind: Commentary available

KEY

C Club Offices
S Club Shop
E Entrance(s) for visiting supporters

↑ North direction (approx)

❶ Bolina Road
❷ South Bermondsey BR
❸ Surrey Quays Underground
❹ Rotherhithe Tunnel
❺ Ilderton Road
❻ The 'Old' Den
❼ River Thames

108

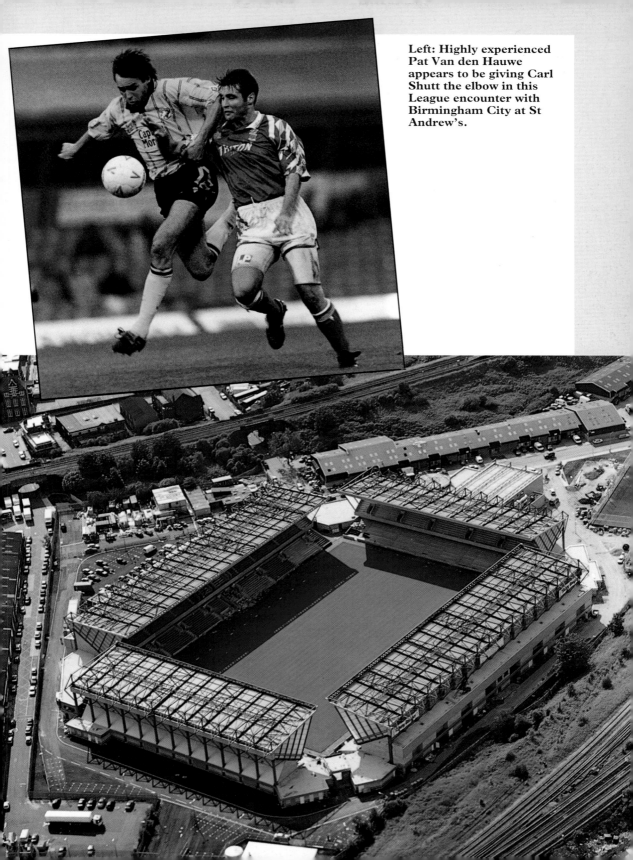

Left: Highly experienced Pat Van den Hauwe appears to be giving Carl Shutt the elbow in this League encounter with Birmingham City at St Andrew's.

NEWCASTLE UNITED

St. James Park, Newcastle-upon-Tyne, NE1 4ST

Tel No: 091 232 8361

Advance Tickets Tel No: 091 261 1571

League: F. A. Premier

Brief History: Founded in 1882 as Newcastle East End, changed to Newcastle United in 1892. Former Grounds: Chillingham Road, moved to St. James Park (former home of defunct Newcastle West End) in 1892. Record attendance 68,386.

(Total) Current Capacity: 32,536 all seated

Club Colours: Black & white striped shirts, black shorts

Nearest Railway Station: Newcastle Central

Parking (Car): Leazes car park & street parking

Parking (Coach/Bus): Leazes car park

Police Force and Tel No: Northumbria (091 232 3451)

Disabled Visitors' Facilities
 Wheelchairs: Sir John Hall Stand
 Blind: Commentary available

KEY

C Club Offices

E Entrance(s) for visiting supporters

S Club Shop

↑ North direction (approx)

❶ St. James Street
❷ Strawberry Place
❸ Gallowgate
❹ Wellington Street
❺ To Newcastle Central BR Station (1/2 mile) & A6127 (M)
❻ Car Park

Right: The prolific goalscoring Andy Cole attracts the personal attentions of the new England coach Bryan Robson.

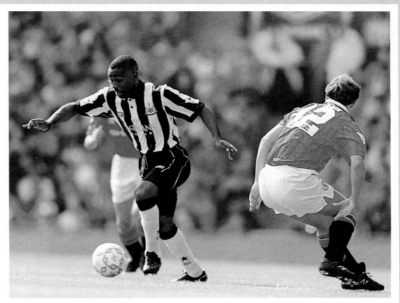

NORTHAMPTON TOWN

County Ground, Abington Avenue, Northampton, NN1 4PS

Tel No: 0604 234100
Advance Tickets Tel No: 0604 234100
League: 3rd Division
Brief History: Founded 1897. Ground is part of Northamptonshire County Cricket Ground. Record attendance 24,523
(Total) Current Capacity: 9,443 (360 Seated)
Club Colours: White with claret trim shirts, white with claret trim shorts
Nearest Railway Station: Northampton Castle
Parking (Car): Street parking
Parking (Coach/Bus): Abington Park
Police Force and Tel No: Northants (0604 33221)

Disabled Visitors' Facilities
   Wheelchairs: Cricket pitch side
   Blind: No special facility
Anticipated Development(s): Re-location to new Council-built Sixfields Stadium during early 1994/95 season. (Editor's note: Work on this ground was not complete by the end of the 1993/94 season, therefore information is incomplete and the photograph relates to the existing County Ground — which is likely to be used early in the 1994/95 season. The new ground rises from an open-field site in the photograph on the facing page.)

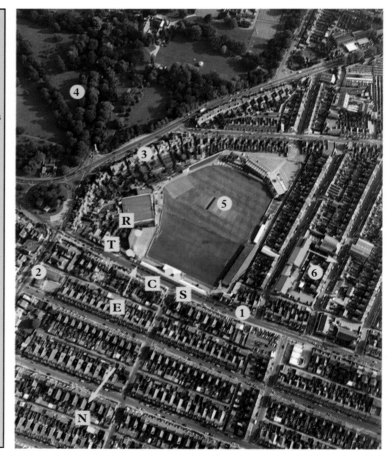

KEY
C Club Offices
S Club Shop
E Entrance(s) for visiting supporters
R Refreshment bars for visiting supporters
T Toilets for visiting supporters

↑ North direction (approx)

❶ Abington Avenue
❷ A5101 Park Avenue North
❸ A45 Wellingborough Road
❹ Park Avenue South
❺ Remainder of County Cricket Ground
❻ Northampton Castle BR Station (2 miles)

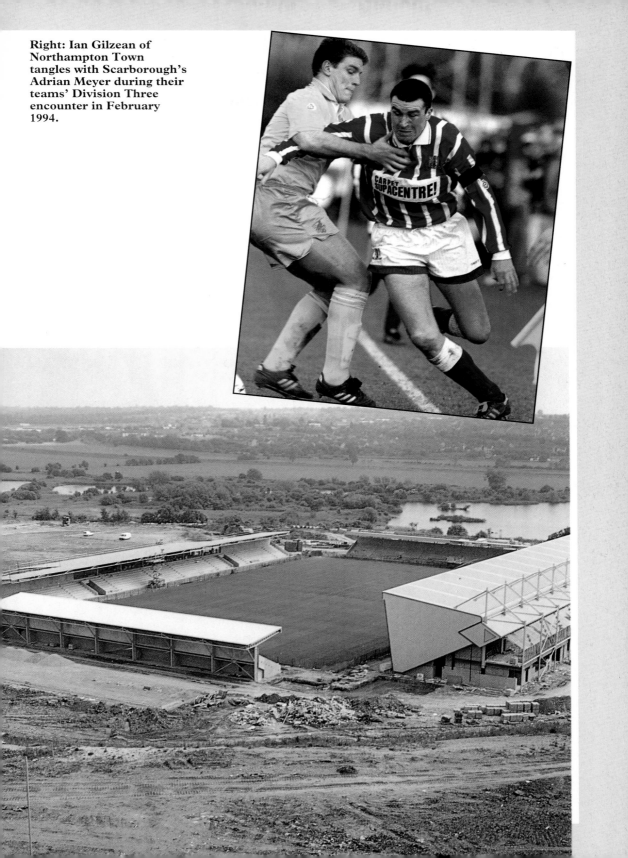

Right: Ian Gilzean of Northampton Town tangles with Scarborough's Adrian Meyer during their teams' Division Three encounter in February 1994.

NORWICH CITY

Carrow Road, Norwich, NR1 1JE

Tel No: 0603 760760
Advance Tickets Tel No: 0603 761661
League: F.A. Premier
Brief History: Founded 1902. Former grounds: Newmarket Road and the Nest, Rosary Road; moved to Carrow Road in 1935. Founder members 3rd Division (1920). Record attendance 43,984.
(Total) Current Capacity: 21,260 Seated

Club Colours: Yellow shirts, green shorts
Nearest Railway Station: Norwich
Parking (Car): City centre car parks
Parking (Coach/Bus): Lower Clarence Road
Police Force and Tel No: Norfolk (0603 621212)
Disabled Visitors' Facilities
  Wheelchairs: South Stand (heated)
  Blind: No special facility

KEY
C Club Offices
S Club Shop
E Entrance(s) for visiting supporters

↑ North direction (approx)

❶ Carrow Road
❷ A47 King Street
❸ River Wensum
❹ Riverside
❺ Car Park
❻ Norwich BR Station

Left: Chris Sutton showing one of the many excellent sides to his all-round game, as he shakes off the close challenge of Spurs' Steve Sedgeley.

NOTTINGHAM FOREST

City Ground, Nottingham, NG2 5FJ

Telephone: 0602 526000
Advance Tickets Telephone: 0602 526002
League: F.A. Premier
Brief History: Founded 1865 as Forest Football Club, changed name to Nottingham Forest (c.1879). Former Grounds: Forest Recreation Ground, Meadow Cricket Ground, Trent Bridge (Cricket Ground), Parkside, Gregory Ground & Town Ground, moved to City Ground in 1898. Founder-members of Second Division (1892). Record attendance 49,045.

(Total) Current Capacity: 28,231 (22,898 Seated)
Club Colours: Red shirts, white shorts
Nearest Railway Station: Nottingham Midland
Parking (Car): East car park & street parking
Parking (Coach/Bus): East car park
Police Force and Tel No: Nottinghamshire (0602 481888)
Disabled Visitors' Facilities
  Wheelchairs: Front of Executive Stand
  Blind: No special facility

KEY

C Club Offices
S Club Shop
E Entrance(s) for visiting supporters

↑ North direction (approx)

❶ Radcliffe Road
❷ Lady Bay Bridge Road
❸ Trent Bridge
❹ Trent Bridge Cricket Ground
❺ Notts County F.C.
❻ River Trent
❼ Nottingham Midland BR Station (1/2 mile)

Left: The highly impressive yet volatile Stan Collymore attempts to rob Birmingham's George Parris during the City Ground fixture in December 1993.

NOTTS COUNTY

Meadow Lane, Nottingham, NG2 3HJ

Tel No: 0602 861155

Advance Tickets Tel No: 0602 850632

League: 1st Division

Brief History: Founded 1862 (oldest club in Football League) as Nottingham, changed to Notts County in c.1882. Former Grounds: Notts Cricket Ground (Beeston), Castle Cricket Ground, Trent Bridge Cricket Ground, moved to Meadow Lane in 1910. Founder-members Football League (1888). Record attendance 47,310.

(Total) Current Capacity: 20,380 Seated

Visiting Supporters Allocation: 5,438 Seated

Club Colours: Black & white stripes, amber sleeves & trim shirts, white shorts.

Nearest Railway Station: Nottingham Midland

Parking (Car): Mainly street parking

Parking (Coach/Bus): Cattle market

Police Force and Tel No: Nottingham (0602 481888)

Disabled Visitors' Facilities
Wheelchairs: County Road/Meadow Lane
Blind: No special facility

Anticipated development(s): Main Stand redevelopment during summer 1994 with probable relocation of club office and club shop.

KEY

C Club Offices

S Club Shop

E Entrance(s) for visiting supporters

R Refreshment bars for visiting supporters

T Toilets for visiting supporters

↑ North direction (approx)

❶ A6011 Meadow Lane
❷ County Road
❸ A60 London Road
❹ River Trent
❺ Nottingham Midland BR Station (¹/₂ mile)

Right: The former Glasgow Rangers player Gary McSwegan now providing the necessary predatory instincts and talent for County in Division One.

OLDHAM ATHLETIC

Boundary Park, Oldham, OL1 2PA

Tel No: 061 624 4972
Advance Tickets Tel No: 061 624 4972
League: 1st Division
Brief History: Founded 1897 as Pine Villa, changed name to Oldham Athletic in 1899. Former Grounds: Berry's Field, Pine Mill, Athletic Ground (later named Boundary Park), Hudson Fold, moved to Boundary Park in 1906. Record attendance 47,671.
(Total) Current Capacity: 16,700 (11,100 Seated)

Club Colours: Blue shirts, blue shorts
Nearest Railway Station: Oldham Werneth
Parking (Car): Lookers Stand car park
Parking (Coach/Bus): At Ground
Police Force and Tel No: Greater Manchester (061 624 0444)
Disabled Visitors' Facilities
    Wheelchairs: Lookers Stand
    Blind: Commentary available

KEY

C Club Offices
E Entrance(s) for visiting supporters

↑ North direction (approx)

❶ A663 Broadway
❷ Furtherwood Road
❸ Chadderton Way
❹ To A627(M) and M62
❺ To Oldham Werneth BR Station (1½ miles)
❻ Car Park

Left: Former team-mates Richard Jobson and Ian Marshall entwined in their attempts to win possession. Oldham seem to have lost some of their punch up front since Marshall became an Ipswich player.

OXFORD UNITED

Manor Ground, London Road, Headington, Oxford, OX3 7RS

Tel No: 0865 61503
Advance Tickets Tel No: 0865 61503
League: 2nd Division
Brief History: Founded 1893 as Headington (later Headington United), changed name to Oxford United in 1960. Former grounds: Brittania Inn Field, Headington Quarry, Wooten's Field, Manor Ground, The Paddocks, moved back to Manor Ground in 1925. Record attendance 22,730.
(Total) Current Capacity: 11,071 (2,777 Seated)

Club Colours: Yellow with navy trim shirts, navy with yellow trim shorts.
Nearest Railway Station: Oxford (3 miles)
Parking (Car): Street parking
Parking (Coach/Bus): Headley Way
Police Force and Tel No: Thames Valley (0865 777501)
Disabled Visitors' Facilities
  Wheelchairs: Beech Road
  Blind: No special facility

KEY

C Club Offices
E Entrance(s) for visiting supporters
R Refreshment bars for visiting supporters

↑ North direction (approx)

❶ A420 London Road
❷ Osler Road
❸ To City Centre and Oxford BR Station (3 miles)
❹ To A40 and Ring Road (¾ mile)
❺ Cuckoo Lane

Right: Much recent interest has been shown in Joey Beauchamp, and it may be that Oxford will be forced to cash in and release him for a hefty fee.

PETERBOROUGH UNITED

London Road, Peterborough, Cambs, PE2 8AL

Tel No: 0733 63947
Advance Tickets Tel No: 0733 63947
League: 2nd Division
Brief History: Founded in 1934, (no connection with former 'Peterborough and Fletton United' FC). Elected to Football League in 1960. Record attendance 30,096.
(Total) Current Capacity: 18,978 (4,715 Seated)

Club Colours: Blue shirts, white shorts
Nearest Railway Station: Peterborough
Parking (Car): At ground
Parking (Coach/Bus): At ground
Police Force and Tel No: Cambridgeshire (0733 63232)
Disabled Visitors' Facilities
    Wheelchairs: London Road End
    Blind: No special facility

KEY
- **C** Club Offices
- **S** Club Shop
- **E** Entrance(s) for visiting supporters
- **R** Refreshment bars for visiting supporters
- **T** Toilets for visiting supporters

↑ North direction (approx)

❶ A15 London Road
❷ Car Parks
❸ Peterborough BR Station (1 mile)
❹ Glebe Road
❺ A605
❻ To A1 (5 miles)

Right: Much travelled Ken Charlery now back in the colours of 'Posh' following his spell at Watford. This ace marksman soon started to hit the back of the net after his return.

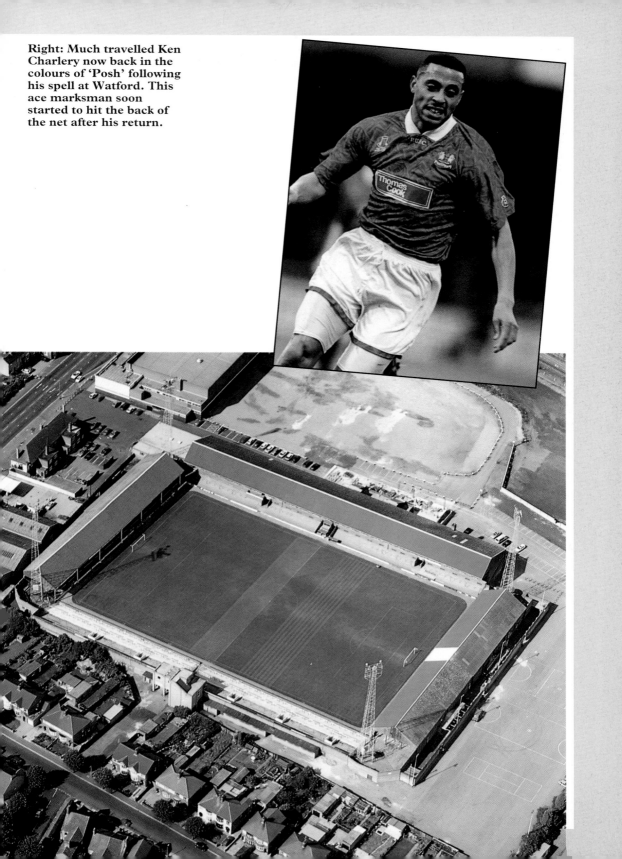

PLYMOUTH ARGYLE

Home Park, Plymouth, PL2 3DQ

Tel No: 0752 562561
Advance Tickets Tel No: 0752 562561
League: 2nd Division
Brief History: Founded 1886 as Argyle Athletic Club, changed name to Plymouth Argyle in 1903. Founder-members Third Division (1920). Record attendance 43,596
(Total) Current Capacity: 19,900 (6,700 Seated)
Club Colours: Green & white striped shirts, black shorts

Nearest Railway Station: Plymouth
Parking (Car): Car park adjacent
Parking (Coach/Bus): Central car park
Police Force and Tel No: Devon & Cornwall (0752 701188)
Disabled Visitors' Facilities
   Wheelchairs: Devonport End
   Blind: Commentary available

KEY
C Club Offices
S Club Shop
E Entrance(s) for visiting supporters
R Refreshment bars for visiting supporters
T Toilets for visiting supporters

↑ North direction (approx)

❶ Outland Road
❷ Car Park
❸ Devonport Road
❹ Central Park
❺ Town Centre & Plymouth BR Station (¾ mile)

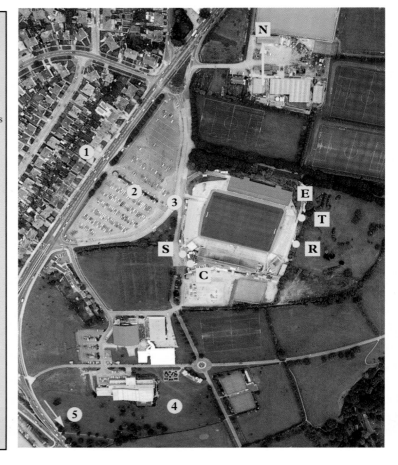

Left: Former Orient favourite Steve Castle, now in Argyle colours, in directive mood, and possibly pointing the way to another three points.

PORTSMOUTH

Fratton Park, 57 Frogmore Road, Portsmouth, Hants, PO4 8RA

Tel No: 0705 731204
Advance Tickets Tel No: 0705 750825
League: 1st Division
Brief History: Founded 1898. Founder-members Third Division (1920). Record attendance 51,385.
(Total) Current Capacity: 26,452 (6,652 Seated)
Visiting Supporters' Allocation: 5,848 (1,228 Seated)
Club Colours: Blue shirts, white shorts

Nearest Railway Station: Fratton
Parking (Car): Street parking
Parking (Coach/Bus): As directed by Police
Police Force and Tel No: Hampshire (0705 321111)
Disabled Visitors' Facilities
    Wheelchairs: Frogmore Road
    Blind: No special facility
Anticipated Development(s): Seeking Ground re-location.

KEY
- **C** Club Offices
- **S** Club Shop
- **E** Entrance(s) for visiting supporters
- **R** Refreshment bars for visiting supporters
- **T** Toilets for visiting supporters

↑ North direction (approx)

- ❶ Alverstone Road
- ❷ Carisbrook Road
- ❸ A288 Milton Road
- ❹ A2030 Eastern Road to A27
- ❺ A2030 Goldsmith Avenue
- ❻ Fratton BR Station (½ mile)

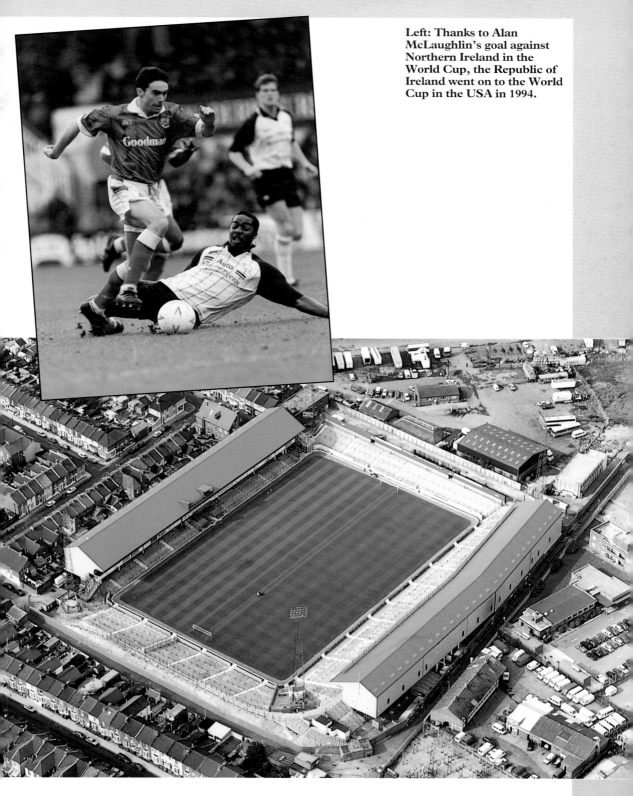

Left: Thanks to Alan McLaughlin's goal against Northern Ireland in the World Cup, the Republic of Ireland went on to the World Cup in the USA in 1994.

PORT VALE

Vale Park, Burslem, Stoke-on-Trent, ST6 1AW

Tel No: 0782 814134
Advance Tickets Tel No: 0782 814134
League: 1st Division
Brief History: Founded 1876 as Burslem Port Vale, changed name to 'Port Vale' in 1907 (reformed club). Former Grounds: The Meadows Longport, Moorland Road Athletic Ground, Cobridge Athletic Grounds, Recreation Ground Hanley, moved to Vale Park in 1950. Founder-members Second Division (1892). Record attendance 50,000.

(Total) Current Capacity: 23,589 (12,442 Seated)
Club Colours: White shirts, black shorts
Nearest Railway Station: Stoke
Parking (Car): Car park at Ground
Parking (Coach/Bus): Hamil Road car park
Police Force and Tel No: Staffordshire (0782 577114)
Disabled Visitors' Facilities
　Wheelchairs: Specialist Stand - Lorne Street
　Blind: Commentary available

KEY

C Club Offices
E Entrance(s) for visiting supporters

↑ North direction (approx)

❶ Car Parks
❷ Hamil Road
❸ Lorne Street
❹ B5051 Moorland Road

Left: Dutchman Robin Van Der Laan, a vital member of the Vale side that achieved promotion just two years after being relegated from the old Division Two.

PRESTON NORTH END

Lowthorpe Road, Deepdale, PR1 6RU

Tel No: 0772 795919
Advance Tickets Tel No: 0772 795919
League: 3rd Division
Brief History: Founded 1867 as a Rugby Club, changed to soccer in 1881. Former ground: Moor park, moved to (later named) Deepdale in 1875. Founder-members Football League (1888). Record attendance 42,684.
(Total) Current Capacity: 16,500 (3,000 Seated)

Club Colours: White shirts, blue shorts
Nearest Railway Station: Preston (2 miles)
Parking (Car): West Stand car park
Parking (Coach/Bus): West Stand car park
Police Force and Tel No: Lancashire (0772 203203)
Disabled Visitors' Facilities
   Wheelchairs: Deepdale Road
   Blind: Earphones Commentary

KEY

C Club Offices
S Club Shop
E Entrance(s) for visiting supporters
R Refreshment bars for visiting supporters
T Toilets for visiting supporters

↑ North direction (approx)

❶ A6033 Deepdale Road
❷ Lawthorpe Road
❸ Car Park
❹ A5085 Blackpool Road
❺ Preston BR Station (2 miles)
❻ Fulwood End – Spion Kop

Left: Preston's Tony Ellis seems to have been around for an eternity but is still a youthful and consistent performer for Preston.

QUEENS PARK RANGERS

Rangers Stadium, South Africa Road, London, W12 7PA

Tel No: 081 743 0262

Tickets and Info. Tel No: 081 749 5744

League: F.A. Premier

Brief History: Founded 1885 as 'St. Jude's Institute', amalgamated with Christchurch Rangers to become Queens Park Rangers in 1886. Football League record number of former Grounds and Ground moves (13 different venues, 17 changes), including White City Stadium (twice) final move to Rangers Stadium (then named Loftus Road) in 1963. Founder-members Third Division (1920). Record attendance 35,353.

(Total) Current Capacity: 19,500 All seated

Club Colours: Blue & white hooped shirts, white shorts

Nearest Railway Station: Shepherds Bush and White City (both tube)

Parking (Car): White City NCP & street parking

Parking (Coach/Bus): White City NCP

Police Force and Tel No: Metropolitan (081 246 2725)

Disabled Visitors Facilities

 Wheelchairs: Ellerslie Road Stand & West Paddock

 Blind: Ellerslie Road Stand

KEY

C Club Offices
S Club Shop
E Entrance(s) for visiting supporters

↑ North direction (approx)

❶ South Africa Road
❷ To White City Tube Station, A219 Wood Lane and A40 Western Avenue
❸ A4020 Uxbridge Road
❹ To Shepherds Bush Tube Station
❺ Ellerslie Road

Left: Les Ferdinand bears down on the Manchester City goal in familiar fashion in this September 1993 Maine Road encounter, while City's Keith Curle attempts to outpace the Rangers man.

READING

Elm Park, Norfolk Road, Reading, RG3 2EF

Tel No: 0734 507878
Advance Tickets Tel No: 0734 507878
League: 1st Division
Brief History: Founded 1871. (Amalgamated with Reading Hornets in 1877 and with Earley in 1889). Former Grounds: Reading Recreation Ground, Reading Cricket Ground, Coley Park and Caversham Cricket Ground, moved to Elm Park in 1895. Founder-members Third Division (1920). Record attendance 33,042.
(Total) Current Capacity: 12,164 (2,100 Seated)
Visiting Supporters Allocation: 3,041 (355 Seated)

Club Colours: White with blue hoops shirts, white shorts
Nearest Railway Station: Reading West
Parking (Car): Street parking & Park & Ride scheme from Prospect School, Honey End Lane.
Parking (Coach/Bus): The Meadway
Police Force and Tel No: Thames Valley (0734 536000)
Disabled Visitors Facilities
  Wheelchairs: Norfolk Road (few)
  Blind: Organised by Hospital Radio

KEY

C Club Offices
S Club Shop
E Entrance(s) for visiting supporters
R Refreshment bars for visiting supporters
T Toilets for visiting supporters

↑ North direction (approx)

❶ Tilehurst Road
❷ Norfolk Road
❸ County Cricket Ground
❹ Reading West BR Station (½ mile)
❺ Liebenrood Road to A4 Bath Road (¼ mile)

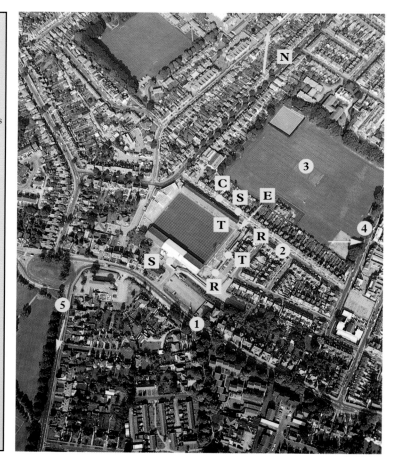

Left: Arguably *the* goalscoring sensation of the 1993/94 season. Nearly forty goals in the League and Cup, and International goals for Northern Ireland, propelled Jimmy Quinn back into the limelight.

ROCHDALE

Willbutts Lane, Spotland, Rochdale, OL11 5DS

Tel No: 0706 44648
Advance Tickets Telephone: 0706 44648
League: 3rd Division
Brief History: Founded 1907 from former Rochdale Town F.C. (founded 1900). Founder-members Third Division North (1921). Record attendance 24,231.
(Total) Current Capacity: 9,000 (2,000 Seated)
Visiting Supporters Allocation: 1,500 (250 Seated)
Club Colours: Blue & white shirts, blue shorts

Nearest Railway Station: Rochdale
Parking (Car): Rear of ground
Parking (Coach/Bus): Rear of ground
Police Force and Tel No: Greater Manchester (0706 47401)
Disabled Visitors' Facilities
   Wheelchairs: Main stand - disabled area
   Blind: No special facility
Anticipated Development(s): Childrens play area planned

KEY

C Club Offices
S Club Shop
E Entrance(s) for visiting supporters
R Refreshment bars for visiting supporters
T Toilets for visiting supporters

↑ North direction (approx)

❶ Willbutts Lane
❷ A627 Edenfield Road
❸ Rochdale BR Station (1/2 mile)
❹ Sandy Lane

Left: Kevin Reid doesn't look too happy with the Deepdale artificial pitch, during the October 1993 fixture with Preston.

ROTHERHAM UNITED

Millmoor Ground, Rotherham, S60 1HR

Tel No: 0709 562434
Advance Tickets Tel No: 0709 562434
League: 2nd Division
Brief History: Founded 1877 (as Thornhill, later Thornhill United), changed name to Rotherham County in 1905 and to Rotherham United in 1925, (amalgamated with Rotherham Town - Football League members 1893-97 - in 1925). Former Grounds include: Red House Ground & Clifton Lane Cricket Ground, moved to Millmoor in 1907. Record attendance 25,000.
(Total) Current Capacity: 14,000 (3,407 Seated)

Visiting Supporters' Allocation: 4,000 (1,000 Seated)
Club Colours: Red shirts, white shorts
Nearest Railway Station: Rotherham Central
Parking (Car): Kimberworth and Main Street car parks, plus large car park adjacent to ground.
Parking (Coach/Bus): As directed by Police
Police Force and Tel No: South Yorkshire (0709 371121)
Disabled Visitors' Facilities
　Wheelchairs: Millmoor Lane
　Blind: No special facility

KEY
- **C** Club Offices
- **S** Club Shop
- **E** Entrance(s) for visiting supporters
- **R** Refreshment bars for visiting supporters
- **T** Toilets for visiting supporters

↑ North direction (approx)

- ❶ Car Park
- ❷ Rotherham Central BR Station
- ❸ A6109 Masborough Road
- ❹ Millmoor Lane
- ❺ To A6178 and M1 Junction 34

**Left: Chris Wilder of
United in action during a
Division Two fixture in
November 1993.**

141

SCARBOROUGH

McCain Stadium, Seamer Road, Scarborough, N. Yorkshire YO12 4HF

Tel No: 0723 375094
Advance Tickets Tel No: 0723 375094
League: 3rd Division
Brief History: Founded 1879 as 'Scarborough Cricketers F.C.' changed name to 'Scarborough F.C.' in 1887. Former grounds: North Marine (Cricket) Ground and Recreation Ground, moved to (then named) Athletic Ground in 1898. Promoted to Football League in 1987. Record attendance 11,124.
(Total) Current Capacity: 8,177 (806 Seated)
Visiting Supporters' Allocation: 2,897 (288 Seated)

Club Colours: Red shirts, white shorts
Nearest Railway Station: Scarborough Central (2 miles)
Parking (Car): Street parking
Parking (Coach/Bus): Weaponess coach/car park
Police Force and Tel No: North Yorkshire (0723 363333)
Disabled Visitors' Facilities
  Wheelchairs: Main Stand, Edgehill Road end.
  Blind: No special facility

KEY

C Club Offices
S Club Shop
E Entrance(s) for visiting supporters
R Refreshment bars for visiting supporters
T Toilets for visiting supporters

↑ North direction (approx)

❶ A64 Seamer Road
❷ Scarborough Central BR Station (2 miles)
❸ To York
❹ McCain Stand

Left: Shaun Murray has just rounded Simon Farnworth of Wigan and looks set to score in this Division Three fixture in December 1993.

SCUNTHORPE UNITED

Glanford Park, Doncaster Road, Scunthorpe DN15 8TD

Tel No: 0724 848077
Advance Tickets Tel No: 0724 848077
League: 3rd Division
Brief History: Founded 1899 as Scunthorpe United, amalgamated with North Lindsey to become 'Scunthorpe & Lindsey United in 1912. Changed name to Scunthorpe United in 1956. Former grounds: Crosby (Lindsey United) & Old Showground, moved to Glanford Park in 1988. Elected to Football League in 1950. Record attendance 8,775 (23,935 at Old Showground).

(Total) Current Capacity: 9,200 (6,400 Seated)
Club Colours: Sky blue shirts with two claret rings on sleeves, white shorts with claret stripe.
Nearest Railway Station: Scunthorpe
Parking (Car): At ground
Parking (Coach/Bus): At ground
Police Force and Tel No: Humberside (0724 282888)
Disabled Visitors' Facilities
  Wheelchairs: Clugston Stand
  Blind: Commentary available

KEY

C Club Offices
S Club Shop
E Entrance(s) for visiting supporters
R Refreshment bars for visiting supporters
T Toilets for visiting supporters

↑ North direction (approx)

❶ Car Park
❷ Glanford Stand
❸ A18 Scunthorpe BR Station and Town Centre (1½ miles)
❹ M181 and M180 Junction 3

Left: United's Graham Atkinson in early season action, in pensive mood, before releasing the ball to a colleague.

SHEFFIELD UNITED

Bramall Lane, Sheffield, S2 4SU

Tel No: 0742 738955
Advance Tickets Tel No: 0742 766771
League: 1st Division
Brief History: Founded 1889. (Sheffield Wednesday occasionally used Bramall Lane c.1880). Founder-members 2nd Division (1892). Record attendance 68,287
(Total) Current Capacity: 23,390 Seated
Visiting Supporters' Allocation: 2,560 Seated
Club Colours: Red & white striped shirts, black shorts

Nearest Railway Station: Sheffield Midland
Parking (Car): Street parking
Parking (Coach/Bus): As directed by Police
Police Force and Tel No: South Yorkshire (0472 768522)
Disabled Visitors' Facilities
  Wheelchairs: (Temporary) South Stand
  Blind: Commentary available

KEY

C Club Offices
E Entrance(s) for visiting supporters
R Refreshment bars for visiting supporters
T Toilets for visiting supporters

↑ North direction (approx)

❶ A621 Bramall Lane
❷ Shoreham Street
❸ Car Park
❹ Sheffield Midland BR Station (¼ mile)
❺ John Street
❻ Spion Kop

146

Left: Ex-'Spurs player David Tuttle – now playing regular first-team football – holds off the attentions of Robert Warzycha of Everton at Brammall Lane in December 1993.

SHEFFIELD WEDNESDAY

Hillsborough, Sheffield, S6 1SW

Tel No: 0742 343122
Advance Tickets Tel No: 0742 337233
League: F.A. Premier
Brief History: Founded 1867 as The Wednesday F.C. (changed to Sheffield Wednesday c.1930). Former Grounds: London Road, Wyrtle Road (Heeley), Sheaf House Ground, Encliffe & Olive Grove (Bramall Lane also used occasionally), moved to Hillsborough (then named 'Owlerton' in 1899). Founder-members Second Division (1892). Record attendance 72,841.
(Total) Current Capacity: 41,237 (23,370 Seated)

Visiting Supporters' Allocation: 4,183 (4,183 Seated)
Club Colours: Blue & white striped shirts, black shorts
Nearest Railway Station: Sheffield (4 miles)
Parking (Car): Street Parking
Parking (Coach/Bus): Owlerton Stadium
Police Force and Tel No: South Yorkshire (0742 343131)
Disabled Visitors' Facilities
   Wheelchairs: North Stand
   Blind: Commentary available

KEY

C Club Offices
S Club Shop
E Entrance(s) for visiting supporters

↑ North direction (approx)

❶ Leppings Lane
❷ River Dom
❸ A61 Penistone Road North
❹ Sheffield BR Station and City Centre (4 miles)
❺ Spion Kop
❻ To M1 (North)
❼ To M1 (South)

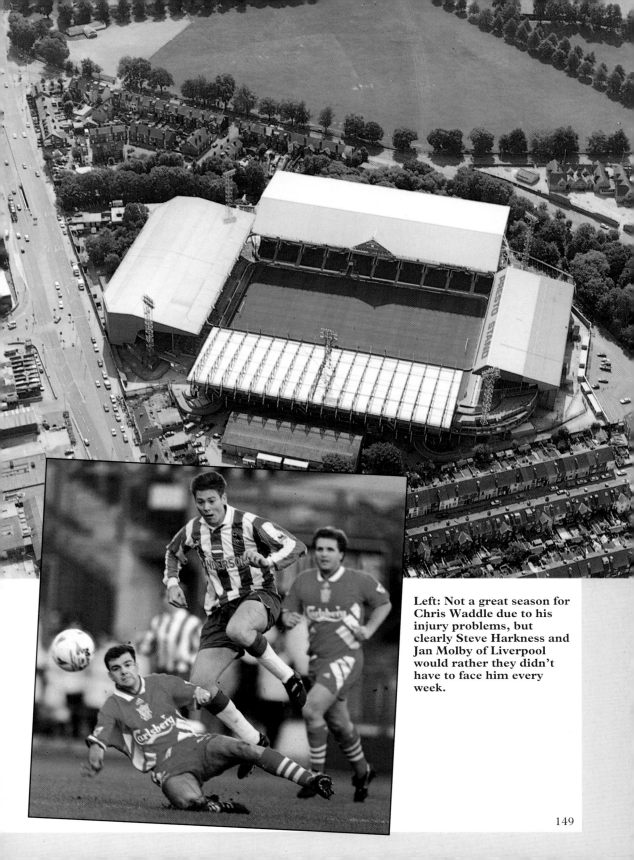

Left: Not a great season for Chris Waddle due to his injury problems, but clearly Steve Harkness and Jan Molby of Liverpool would rather they didn't have to face him every week.

SHREWSBURY TOWN

Gay Meadow, Shrewsbury, SY2 6AB

Tel No: 0743 360111
Advance Tickets Tel No: 0743 360111
League: 2nd Division
Brief History: Founded 1886. Former Grounds: Monkmoor Racecourse, Ambler's Field & The Barracks Ground (moved to Gay Meadow in 1910). Elected to Football League in 1950. Record attendance 18,917
(Total) Current Capacity: 8,000 (3,000 Seated)
Club Colours: Blue with White collar shirts, blue shorts.

Nearest Railway Station: Shrewsbury
Parking (Car): Adjacent car park
Parking (Coach/Bus): Gay Meadow
Police Force and Tel No: West Mercia (0743 232888)
Disabled Visitors' Facilities
   Wheelchairs: Alongside Pitch (as directed)
   Blind: No special facility
Anticipated Development(s): Re-furbishment of present ground.

KEY
C Club Offices
S Club Shop
E Entrance(s) for visiting supporters
R Refreshment bars for visiting supporters
T Toilets for visiting supporters

⬆ North direction (approx)

❶ Entrance road to ground
❷ Abbey Foregate
❸ River Severn
❹ Car Parks
❺ Shrewsbury BR Station (1 mile — shortest route)
❻ Riverside enclosure

Right: Michael Brown has his work cut out avoiding the attentions of Wycombe's Steve Guppy, in this November 1993 Division Three clash at Adams Park.

SOUTHAMPTON

The Dell, Milton Road, Southampton, SO9 4XX

Tel No: 0703 220505

Advance Tickets Tel No: 0703 228575

League: F.A. Premier

Brief History: Founded 1885 as 'Southampton St. Mary's Young Mens Association' (changed name to Southampton in 1897). Former Grounds: Northlands Road, Antelope Ground, County Ground, moved to The Dell in 1898. Founder-members Third Division (1920). Record attendance 31,044.

(Total) Current Capacity: 21,909 (8,808 Seated)

Visiting Supporters' Allocation: 2,438 (526 Seated)

Club Colours: Red & white shirts, black shorts

Nearest Railway Station: Southampton

Parking (Car): Street parking

Parking (Coach/Bus): As directed by Police

Police Force and Tel No: Hampshire (0703 581111)

Disabled Visitors' Facilities
Wheelchairs: Milton Road (book in advance)
Blind: Commentary available (book in advance)

Anticipated Development(s): The Milton Road end will be seated and rooted for the start of the 1994/95 season.

KEY

C Club Offices

S Club Shop

E Entrance(s) for visiting supporters

R Refreshment bars for visiting supporters

T Toilets for visiting supporters

↑ North direction (approx)

❶ Archers Road
❷ Milton Road
❸ Southampton BR Station
❹ Hill Lane

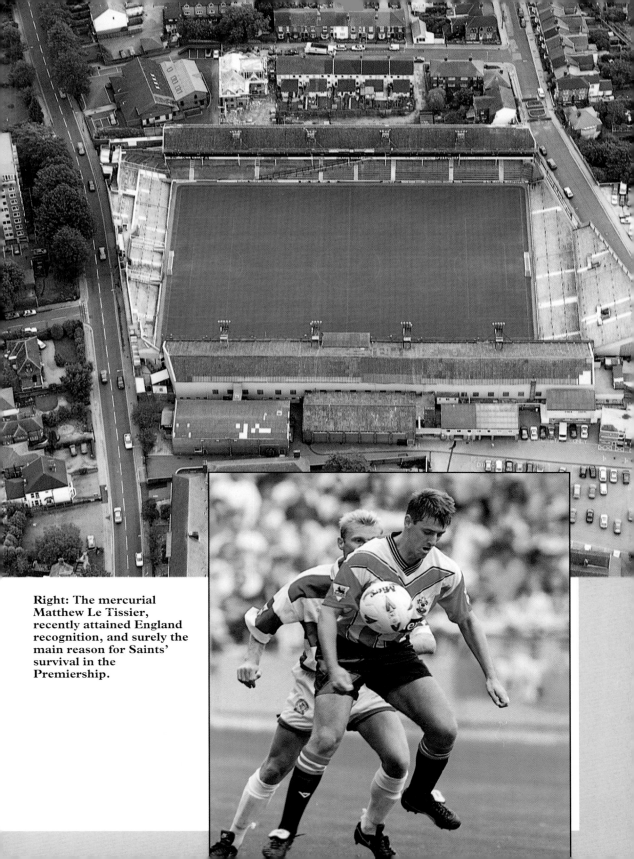

Right: The mercurial Matthew Le Tissier, recently attained England recognition, and surely the main reason for Saints' survival in the Premiership.

SOUTHEND UNITED

Roots Hall Ground, Victoria Avenue, Southend-on-Sea, SS2 6NQ

Tel No: 0702 340707
Advance Tickets Tel No: 0702 435602
League: 1st Division
Brief History: Founded 1906. Former Grounds: Roots Hall, Kursaal, The Stadium Grainger Road, moved to Roots Hall (new Ground) 1955. Founder-members Third Division (1920). Record attendance 31,033.
(Total) Current Capacity: 13,332

Club Colours: Blue with yellow trim shirts, yellow shorts
Nearest Railway Station: Prittlewell
Parking (Car): Street parking
Parking (Coach/Bus): Car park at Ground
Police Force and Tel No: Essex (0702 431212)
Disabled Visitors' Facilities
    Wheelchairs: West Stand
    Blind: Commentary available

KEY

C Club Offices
E Entrance(s) for visiting supporters

↑ North direction (approx)

❶ Director's Car Park
❷ Prittlewell BR Station (¼ mile)
❸ A127 Victoria Avenue
❹ Fairfax Drive
❺ Southend centre (½ mile)
❻ North Bank

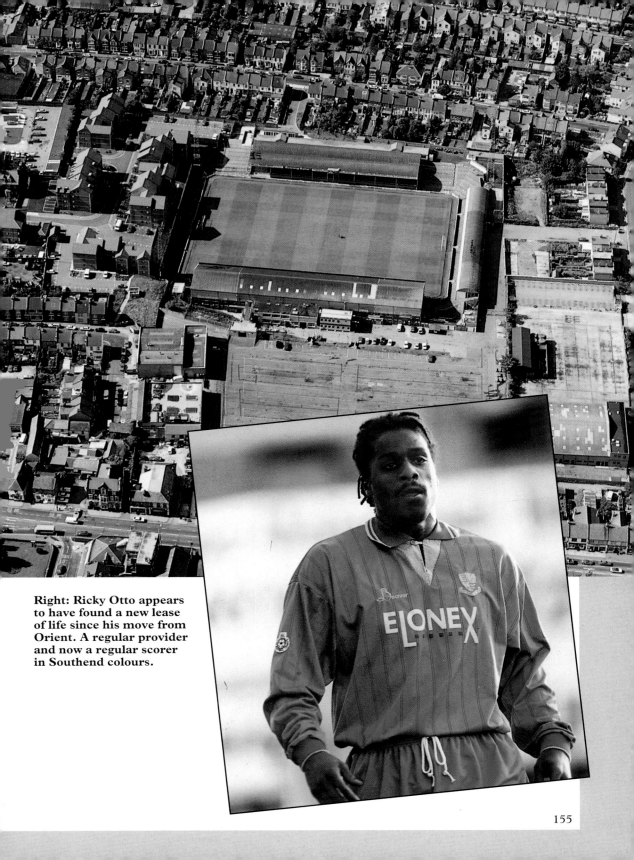

Right: Ricky Otto appears to have found a new lease of life since his move from Orient. A regular provider and now a regular scorer in Southend colours.

STOCKPORT COUNTY

Edgeley Park, Hardcastle Road, Edgeley, Stockport, SK3 9DD

Tel No: 061 480 8888
Advance Tickets Tel No: 061 480 8888
League: 2nd Division
Brief History: Founded 1883 as Heaton Norris Rovers, changed name to Stockport County in 1890. Former Grounds: Heaton Norris Recreation Ground, Heaton Norris Wanderers Cricket Ground, Chorlton's Farm, Ash Inn Ground, Wilkes Field (Belmont Street) and Nursery Inn (Green Lane), moved to Edgeley Park in 1902. Record attendance 27,833.
(Total) Current Capacity: 8,020 (4,200 Seated)

Club Colours: Blue shirts with red & white flashes, white shorts
Nearest Railway Station: Stockport
Parking (Car): Street parking
Parking (Coach/Bus): As directed by Police
Police Force and Tel No: Greater Manchester (061 872 5050)
Disabled Visitors' Facilities
  Wheelchairs: Main Stand
  Blind: Headsets available

KEY

C Club Offices
E Entrance(s) for visiting supporters
R Refreshment bars for visiting supporters
T Toilets for visiting supporters

↑ North direction (approx)

❶ Mercian Way
❷ Hardcastle Road
❸ Stockport BR Station (¼ mile)
❹ Railway End
❺ Main Stand

156

Left: The tall Kevin Francis and just half of a superb partnership (with Andy Preece), which produced over 50 goals, and was instrumental in guiding County to the Play-offs again.

STOKE CITY

Victoria Ground, Boothen Old Road, Stoke-on-Trent, ST4 4EG

Tel No: 0782 413511
Advance Tickets Tel No: 0782 413961
League: 1st Division
Brief History: Founded 1863 as Stoke F.C., amalgamated with Stoke Victoria in 1878, changed to Stoke City in 1925. Former Ground: Sweetings Field, moved to Victoria Ground in 1878. Founder-members Football League (1888). Record attendance 51,380.
(Total) Current Capacity: 25,259 (9,625 Seated)

Club Colours: Red & white striped shirts, white shorts
Nearest Railway Station: Stoke-on-Trent
Parking (Car): Car park at ground
Parking (Coach/Bus): Whieldon Road
Police Force and Tel No: Staffordshire (0784 744644)
Disabled Visitors' Facilities
  Wheelchairs: Corner Butler Street/Boothen End
  Blind: Limited facilities (contact first)

KEY

C Club Offices
S Club Shop
E Entrance(s) for visiting supporters

↑ North direction (approx)

❶ Car Park
❷ Campbell Road
❸ A500 Queensway
❹ M6 Junction 15 (4 miles via A500)
❺ Stoke-on-Trent BR Station (½ mile)

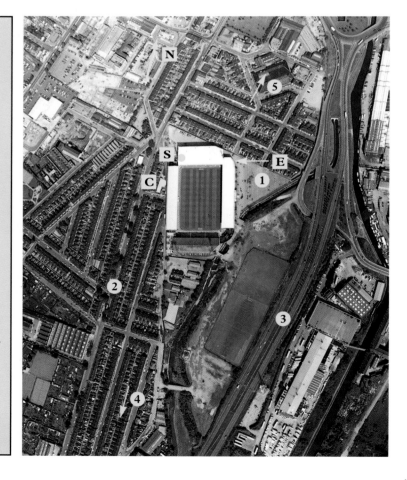

Left: Simon Sturridge appears to have the ball attached to his foot in this picture. This speedy winger has settled well since his move from Birmingham.

SUNDERLAND

Roker Park, Grantham Road, Roker, Sunderland, SR6 9SW

Tel No: 091 514 0332
Advance Tickets Tel No: 091 514 0332
League: 1st Division
Brief History: Founded 1879 as 'Sunderland and District Teachers Association', changed to 'Sunderland Association' (in 1880) and shortly after to 'Sunderland'. Former Grounds: Blue House Field, Groves Field (Ashbrooke), Horatio Street, Abbs Field & Newcastle Road, moved to Roker Park in 1898. Record attendance 75,118
(Total) Current Capacity: 27,763 (7,753 Seated)

Club Colours: Red & white striped shirts, black shorts
Nearest Railway Station: Seaburn
Parking (Car): Car park adjacent ground
Parking (Coach/Bus): Seafront, Roker
Police Force and Tel No: Northumbria (091 567 6155)
Disabled Visitors' Facilities
 Wheelchairs: Roker Baths Road
 Blind: Commentary available
Anticipated Development(s): Possible move to new 48,000 all-seater Stadium, 1995/96 season.

KEY

C Club Offices
S Club Shop
E Entrance(s) for visiting supporters

↑ North direction (approx)

❶ Roker Baths Road
❷ Grantham Road
❸ Seaburn BR Station (1 mile)
❹ To A1018 Newcastle Road
❺ Hampden Road
❻ To A183 Roker Terrace (Seafront)
❼ Car Park

Left: Another target for the so-called big clubs, former Luton favourite Phil Gray showing fine close control in his adopted Sunderland colours at Roker Park.

SWANSEA CITY

Vetch Field, Swansea, SA1 3SU

Tel No: 0792 474114
Advance Tickets Tel No: 0792 474114
League: 2nd Division
Brief History: Founded 1900 as Swansea Town, changed to Swansea City in 1970. Former Grounds: various, including Recreation Ground. Moved to Vetch Field in 1912. Founder-members Third Division (1920). Record attendance 32,796.
(Total) Current Capacity: 16,419 (3,414 Seated)
Club Colours: White shirts, white shorts
Nearest Railway Station: Swansea High Street

Parking (Car): Kingsway car park & adjacent Clarence Terrace, (supervised car park).
Parking (Coach/Bus): As directed by Police
Police Force and Tel No: South Wales (0792 456999)
Disabled Visitors' Facilities
  Wheelchairs: Glamorgan Street
  Blind: No special facility
Anticipated Development(s): New 6,500 seated Stand on North Bank and new dressing rooms, community hall and offices. (Editor's note: Updated information regarding ground not advised.)

KEY

C Club Offices
S Club Shop
E Entrance(s) for visiting supporters

↑ North direction (approx)

❶ Glamorgan Street
❷ William Street
❸ Richardson Street
❹ A4067 Oystermouth Road (8 miles to M4 Junction 42)
❺ Swansea High Street BR Station (1/2 mile)
❻ Supervised Car Park
❼ North Bank

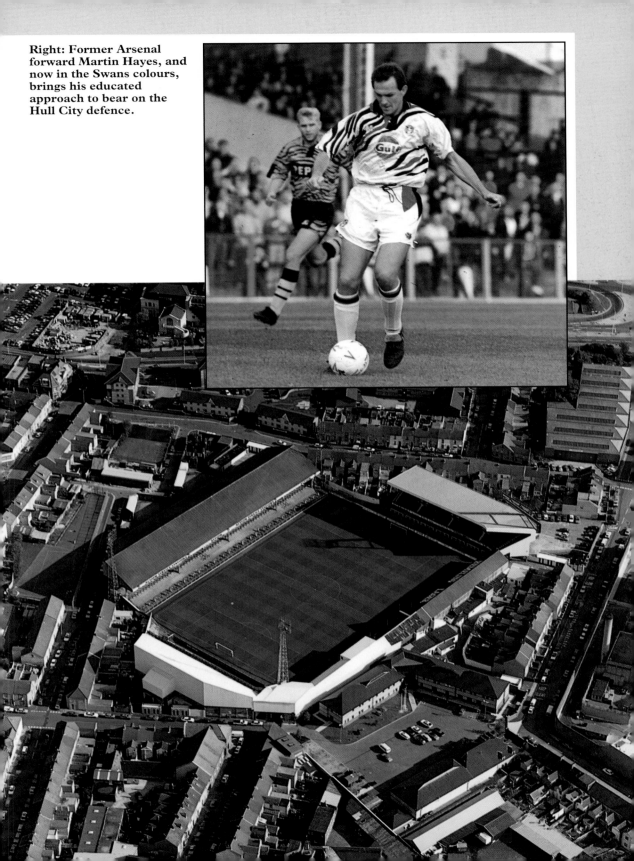

Right: Former Arsenal forward Martin Hayes, and now in the Swans colours, brings his educated approach to bear on the Hull City defence.

SWINDON TOWN

County Ground, County Road, Swindon, SN1 2ED

Tel No: 0793 430430

Advance Tickets Tel No: 0793 430430

League: 1st Division

Brief History: Founded 1881. Former Grounds: Quarry Ground, Globe Field, Croft Ground, County Ground (adjacent current to Ground and now Cricket Ground), moved to current County Ground in 1896. Founder-members Third Division (1920). Record attendance 32,000

(Total) Current Capacity: 19,000 all seater when new Stands complete

Visiting Supporters Allocation: 1,000 Seated (3,000 when new Stand complete)

Club Colours: Red shirts, red shorts

Nearest Railway Station: Swindon

Parking (Car): Town Centre

Parking (Coach/Bus): Adjacent car park

Police Force and Tel No: Wiltshire (0793 528111)

Disabled Visitors Facilities
  Wheelchairs: Intel Stand
  Blind: Commentary available

Anticipated Development(s): New Stratton Bank Stand, end of 1994/95 season.

KEY

C Club Offices
S Club Shop
E Entrance(s) for visiting supporters
R Refreshment bars for visiting supporters
T Toilets for visiting supporters

↑ North direction (approx)

❶ Shrivenham Road
❷ County Road
❸ A345 Queens Drive (M4 Junction 15 – 3½ miles)
❹ Swindon BR Station (½ mile)
❺ Town End
❻ Car Park
❼ County Cricket Ground

Right: In a season of many disappointments, Shaun Taylor gets the better of Villa's Andy Townsend on this occasion. A consistent defender during troubled times.

TORQUAY UNITED

Plainmoor Ground, Torquay, TQ1 3PS

Tel No: 0803 328666
Advance Tickets Tel No: 0803 328666
League: 3rd Division
Brief History: Founded 1898, as Torquay United, amalgamated with Ellacombe in 1910, changed name to Torquay Town. Amalgamated with Babbacombe in 1921, changed name to Torquay United. Former grounds: Teignmouth Road, Torquay Recreation Ground, Cricketfield Road & Torquay Cricket Ground, moved to Plainmoor (Ellacombe Ground) in 1910. Record attendance 21,908.
(Total) Current Capacity: 6,455 (2,324 Seated)
Visiting Supporters' Allocation: 1,248 (200 Seated)

Club Colours: Yellow with navy & white stripe shirts, navy shorts

Nearest Railway Station: Torquay (2 miles)

Parking (Car): Street parking

Parking (Coach/Bus): Lymington Road coach station

Police Force and Tel No: Devon & Cornwall (0803 214491)

Disabled Visitors Facilities
Wheelchairs: Main Office
Blind: Commentary available

KEY
C Club Offices
S Club Shop
E Entrance(s) for visiting supporters
R Refreshment bars for visiting supporters
T Toilets for visiting supporters

⬆ North direction (approx)

❶ Warbro Road
❷ B3202 Marychurch Road
❸ Marnham Road
❹ Torquay BR Station (2 miles)

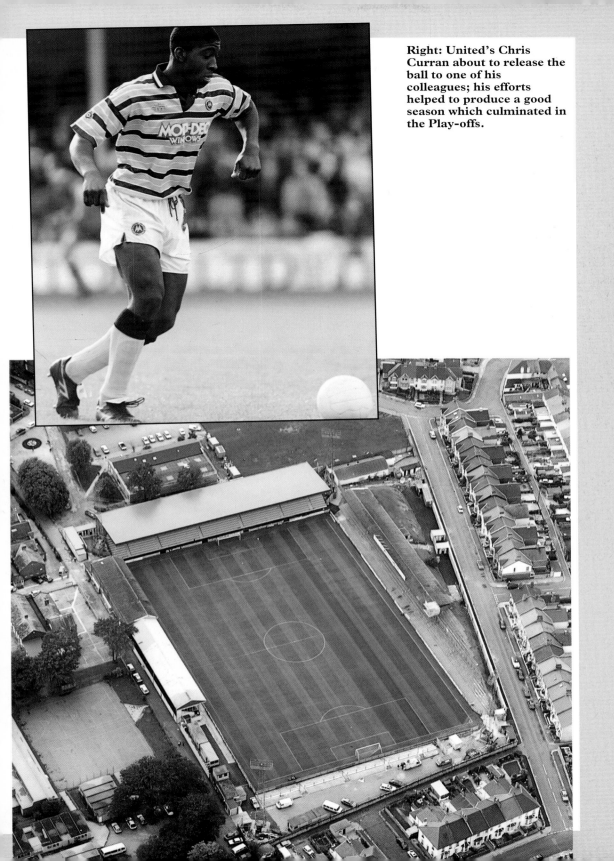

Right: United's Chris Curran about to release the ball to one of his colleagues; his efforts helped to produce a good season which culminated in the Play-offs.

TOTTENHAM HOTSPUR

White Hart Lane, 748 High Road, Tottenham, London N17 0AP

Tel No: 081 808 6666
Advance Tickets Tel No: 081 808 8080
League: F. A. Premier
Brief History: Founded 1882 as 'Hotspur', changed name to Tottenham Hotspur in 1885. Former Grounds: Tottenham Marshes and Northumberland Park, moved to White Hart Lane in 1899. F. A. Cup winner 1901 (as a non-League club). Record attendance 75,038
(Total) Current Capacity: 33,740 (25,883 Seated)
Visiting Supporters' Allocation: 2,481 (2,481 Seated – maximum)
Club Colours: White shirts, navy blue shorts

Nearest Railway Station: White Hart Lane plus Seven Sisters & Manor House (tube)
Parking (Car): Street parking (min ¼ mile from ground)
Parking (Coach/Bus): Northumberland Park coach park
Police Force and Tel No: Metropolitan (081 801 3443)
Disabled Visitors' Facilities
   Wheelchairs: Paxton Road and High Road (by prior arrangement)
   Blind: No special facility

KEY	
C	Club Offices
S	Club Shop
E	Entrance(s) for visiting supporters
R	Refreshment bars for visiting supporters
T	Toilets for visiting supporters

↑ North direction (approx)

❶ Park Lane
❷ A1010 High Road
❸ White Hart Lane BR Station
❹ Paxton Road
❺ Worcester Avenue
❻ West Stand

Left: Darren Anderton turns on the style in this Premiership encounter with Norwich in December 1993. England honours were to follow shortly afterwards.

TRANMERE ROVERS

Prenton Park, Prenton Road West, Birkenhead, L42 9PN

Tel No: 051 608 3677
Advance Tickets Tel No: 051 608 3677
League: 1st Division
Brief History: Founded 1884 as Belmont F.C., changed name to Tranmere Rovers in 1885 (not connected to earlier 'Tranmere Rovers'). Former grounds: Steele's Field and Ravenshaw's Field (also known as Old Prenton Park, ground of Tranmere Rugby Club), moved to (new) Prenton Park in 1911. Founder-members 3rd Division North (1921). Record attendance 24,424.
(Total) Current Capacity: 17,452 (3,800 Seated)

Visiting Supporters' Allocation: 3,960 (368 Seated)
Club Colours: White shirts, white shorts
Nearest Railway Station: Hamilton Square or Rock Ferry
Parking (Car): Car park at Ground
Parking (Coach/Bus): Car park at Ground
Police Force and Tel No: Merseyside (051 709 6010)
Disabled Visitors' Facilities
  Wheelchairs: Main Stand
  Blind: No special facility

KEY

C Club Offices
S Club Shop
E Entrance(s) for visiting supporters
R Refreshment bars for visiting supporters
T Toilets for visiting supporters

↑ North direction (approx)

❶ Car Park
❷ Prenton Road West
❸ Borough Road
❹ M53 Junction 4 (B5151) – 3 miles
❺ Birkenhead (1 mile)

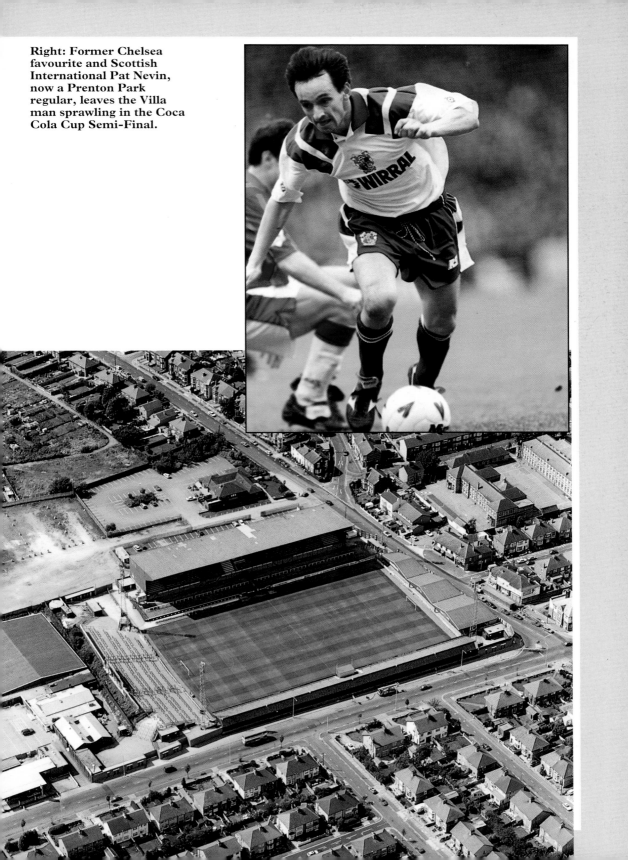

Right: Former Chelsea favourite and Scottish International Pat Nevin, now a Prenton Park regular, leaves the Villa man sprawling in the Coca Cola Cup Semi-Final.

WALSALL

Bescot Stadium, Bescot Crescent, Walsall, West Midlands, WS1 4SA

Tel No: 0922 22791
Advance Tickets Tel No: 0922 22791
League: 3rd Division
Brief History: Founded 1888 as Walsall Town Swifts (amalgamation of Walsall Town - founded 1884 - and Walsall Swifts - founded 1885), changed name to Walsall in 1895. Former Grounds: The Chuckery, West Bromwich Road (twice), Hilary Street (later named Fellows Park, twice), moved to Bescot Stadium in 1990. Founder-members Second Division (1892). Record attendance 10,628 (24,100 at Fellows Park).

(Total) Current Capacity: 9,485 (6,685 Seated)
Visiting Supporters' Allocation: 1,916 (1,916 Seated)
Club Colours: Red shirts, White shorts
Nearest Railway Station: Bescot
Parking (Car): Car park at Ground
Parking (Coach/Bus): Car park at Ground
Police Force and Tel No : West Midlands (0922 38111)
Disabled Visitors' Facilities
  Wheelchairs: Highgate Stand
  Blind: Commentary planned

KEY

C Club Offices
S Club Shop
E Entrance(s) for visiting supporters
R Refreshment bars for visiting supporters
T Toilets for visiting supporters

↑ North direction (approx)

❶ Motorway M6
❷ M6 Junction 9
❸ Bescot BR Station
❹ Car Parks
❺ Bescot Crescent

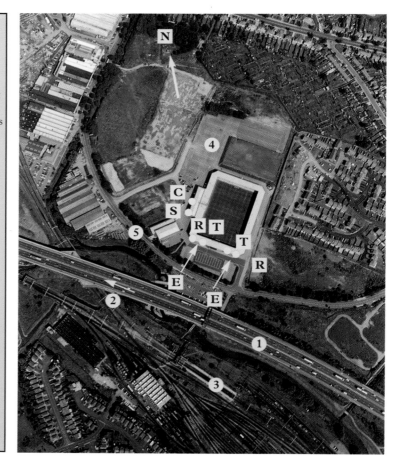

Left: Evran Wright seems to have overrun the ball in his efforts to get on the scoresheet again, in the fixture versus Mansfield at Field Mill.

WATFORD

Vicarage Road Stadium, Watford, WD1 8ER

Tel No: 0923 230933
Advance Tickets Tel No: 0923 220393
League: 1st Division
Brief History: Founded 1898 as an amalgamation of West Herts (founded 1891) and Watford St. Mary's (founded early 1890s). Former Grounds: Wiggenhall Road (Watford St. Mary's) and West Herts Sports Ground, moved to Vicarage Road in 1922. Founder-members Third Division (1920). Record attendance 34,099.
(Total) Current Capacity: 16,000 (Anticipated 1994/95 season)
Club Colours: Yellow shirts with black collar & shoulder panel, Black shorts with yellow & red trim.

Nearest Railway Station: Watford High Street or Watford Junction.
Parking (Car): Nearby multi-storey car park in town centre (10 mins walk)
Parking (Coach/Bus): Cardiff Road car park
Police Force and Tel No: Hertfordshire (0923 244444)
Disabled Visitors Facilities
　Wheelchairs: Corner East Stand and South Terrace (special enclosure for approx. 20 wheelchairs), plus enclosure in North East Corner
　Blind: Commentary available in the East Stand (20 seats, free of charge)
Anticipated Development(s): New Stand at South End (Late 1994)

KEY

C Club Offices
S Club Shop
E Entrance(s) for visiting supporters
R Refreshment bars for visiting supporters

↑ North direction (approx)

❶ Vicarage Road
❷ Occupation Road
❸ Rous Stand
❹ Town Centre (1/2 mile) – Car Parks, High Street BR Station
❺ Watford West BR Station

174

Right: Watford midfielder Andy Hessenthaler, probably one of the hardest working and most consistent players in the Endsleigh League.

WEST BROMWICH ALBION

The Hawthorns, Halfords Lane, West Bromwich, West Midlands, B71 4LF

Tel No: 021 525 8888

Advance Tickets Tel No: 021 553 5472

League: 1st Division

Brief History: Founded 1879. Former Grounds: Coopers Hill, Dartmouth Park, Four Acres, Stoney Lane, moved to the Hawthorns in 1900. Founder-members of Football League (1888). Record attendance 64,815.

(Total) Current Capacity: 26,000 all seated from Dec. 1994

Club Colours: Navy blue & white striped shirts, white shorts

Nearest Railway Station: Rolfe Street, Smethwick (1½ miles)

Parking (Car): Halfords Lane & Rainbow Stand car parks.

Parking (Coach/Bus): Rainbow Stand car park

Police Force and Tel No: West Midlands (021 554 3414)

Disabled Visitors' Facilities
Wheelchairs: Corner Birmingham Road/Main Stand
Blind: Facility available

Anticipated Development(s): Re-development of Smethwick End, and Birmingham Road End, late 1994.

KEY

C Club Offices
S Club Shop
E Entrance(s) for visiting supporters
T Toilets for visiting supporters

↑ North direction (approx)

❶ A41 Birmingham Road
❷ M5 Junction 1 (¾ mile)
❸ Birmingham centre (4 miles)
❹ Halfords Lane
❺ Main Stand
❻ Smethwick End
❼ Rolfe Street, Smethwick BR Station (1½ miles)

Left: A familiar sight to Baggies fans, Bob Taylor finds the net yet again, this time Derby County are on the receiving end at The Baseball Ground.

WEST HAM UNITED

Boleyn Ground, Green Street, Upton Park, London, E13 9AZ

Tel No: 081 472 2740
Advance Tickets Tel No: 081 472 3322
League: F. A. Premier
Brief History: Founded 1895 as Thames Ironworks, changed name to West Ham United in 1900. Former Grounds: Hermit Road, Browning Road, The Memorial Ground, moved to Boleyn Ground in 1904. Record attendance 42,322.
(Total) Current Capacity: 22,503 (11,600 Seated)
Visiting Supporters' Allocation: 3,000 (500 Seated)
Club Colours: Claret & blue shirts, white shorts.

Nearest Railway Station: Barking BR, Upton Park (tube)

Parking (Car): Street parking

Parking (Coach/Bus): As directed by police

Police Force and Tel No: Metropolitan (081 593 8232)

Disabled Visitors' Facilities
  Wheelchairs: Green Street
  Blind: No special facility

Development(s): (Editor's note: Updated information regarding ground not advised.)

KEY

C Club Offices
S Club Shop
E Entrance(s) for visiting supporters
R Refreshment bars for visiting supporters
T Toilets for visiting supporters

↑ North direction (approx)

❶ A124 Barking Road
❷ Green Street
❸ North Bank
❹ Upton Park Tube Station (¼ mile)
❺ Barking BR Station (1 mile)

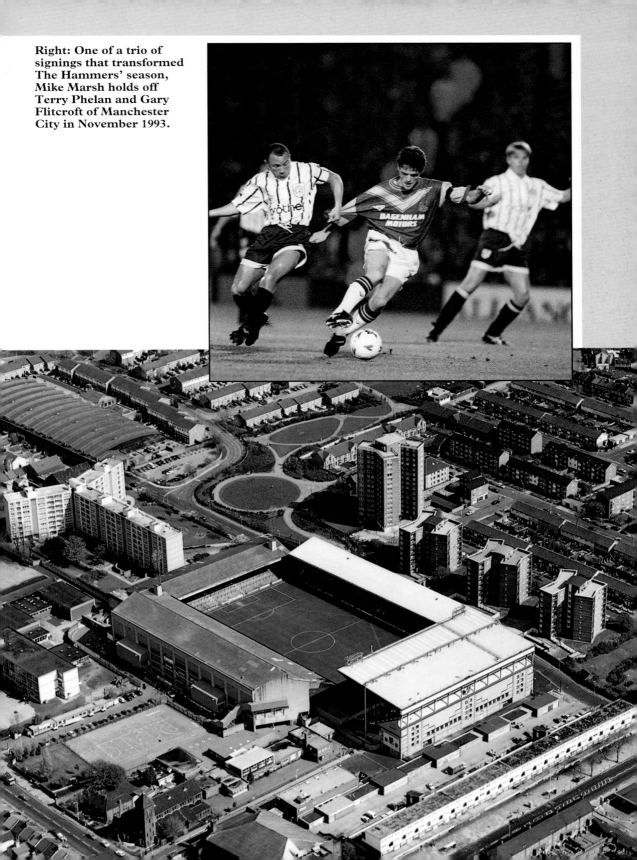

Right: One of a trio of signings that transformed The Hammers' season, Mike Marsh holds off Terry Phelan and Gary Flitcroft of Manchester City in November 1993.

WIGAN ATHLETIC

Springfield Park, Wigan, Lancs, WN6 7BA

Tel No: 0942 44433
Advance Tickets Tel No: 0942 44433
League: 3rd Division
Brief History: Founded 1932. Springfield Park used by former club Wigan Borough (Football League 1921-31) but unrelated to current club. Elected to Football League in 1978 (the last club to be elected rather than promoted). Record attendance 27,500.
(Total) Current Capacity: 4,359 (1,109 Seated)
Visiting Supporters Allocation: 1,500 (300 Seated)

Club Colours: Royal Blue & Black stripes shirt, black shorts
Nearest Railway Station: Wallgate and North Western (1 mile)
Parking (Car): Street parking
Parking (Coach/Bus): At Ground
Police Force and Tel No: Greater Manchester (0942 44981)
Disabled Visitors' Facilities
  Wheelchairs: Phoenix Stand side
  Blind: Commentary available

KEY
C Club Offices
S Club Shop
E Entrance(s) for visiting supporters
R Refreshment bars for visiting supporters
T Toilets for visiting supporters

↑ North direction (approx)

❶ Private Car Park
❷ Springfield Road
❸ St. Andrews Drive
❹ Wallgate and North Western BR Stations (1 mile)
❺ B5375 Woodhouse Lane

Left: Goalie Simon Farnworth dusts himself down after another fine save at Springfield Park. His efforts helped avoid an even worse 1993/94 season for the Athletic.

WIMBLEDON

Selhurst Park, London, SE25 6PU

Tel No: 081 771 2233
Advance Tickets Tel No: 081 771 8841
League: F.A. Premier
Brief History: Founded 1889 as Wimbledon Old Centrals, changed name to Wimbledon in 1905. Former Grounds: Wimbledon Common, Pepy's Road, Grand Drive, Merton Hall Road, Malden Wanderers Cricket Ground & Plough Lane. Moved to Selhurst Park (Crystal Palace F.C. Ground) in 1991. Elected to Football League in 1977. Record attendance (Plough Lane) 18,000.
(Total) Current Capacity: 17,625 all Seated (For two seasons only whilst new Holmesdale Road Stand is being built)

Visiting Supporters Allocation: 2,337 Anticipated
Club Colours: Blue shirts, blue shorts
Nearest Railway Station: Selhurst, Norwood Junction & Thornton Heath
Parking (Car): Street parking & Sainsbury's car park
Parking (Coach/Bus): Thornton Heath
Police Force and Tel No: Metropolitan (081 649 1391)
Disabled Visitors Facilities
  Wheelchairs: Park Road
  Blind: Commentary available
Anticipated Development(s): New Stand Holmesdale Road end.

KEY

C Club Offices
S Club Shop
E Entrance(s) for visiting supporters
R Refreshment bars for visiting supporters
T Toilets for visiting supporters

↑ North direction (approx)

❶ Whitehorse Lane
❷ Park Road
❸ A213 Selhurst Road
❹ Selhurst BR Station (1/2 mile)
❺ Norwood Junction BR Station
❻ Thornton Heath BR Station (1/2 mile)
❼ Car Park (Sainsbury's)

Right: Prolific scorer with Brentford in the lower divisions, and now with The Dons in the top flight. International honours may not be far away for Dean Holdsworth.

WOLVERHAMPTON WANDERERS

Molineux Ground, Waterloo Road, Wolverhampton, WV1 4QR

Tel No: 0902 712181
Advance Tickets Tel No: 0902 25899
League: 1st Division
Brief History: Founded 1877 as St. Lukes, combined with Goldthorn Hill to become Wolverhampton Wanderers in 1884. Former Grounds: Old Windmill Field, John Harper's Field and Dudley Road, moved to Molineux in 1889. Founder-members Football League (1888). Record attendance 61,315
(Total) Current Capacity: 19,300 (14,300 Seated)
Club Colours: Gold shirts, black shorts

Nearest Railway Station: Wolverhampton
Parking (Car): West Park and adjacent North Bank
Parking (Coach/Bus): As directed by Police
Police Force and Tel No: West Midlands (0902 27851)
Disabled Visitors' Facilities
  Wheelchairs: North Bank
  Blind: Commentary (by prior arrangement).
Anticipated Development(s): (Editor's note: Updated information regarding ground not advised.)

KEY

C Club Offices
S Club Shop
E Entrance(s) for visiting supporters
R Refreshment bars for visiting supporters
T Toilets for visiting supporters

↑ North direction (approx)

❶ Stan Cullis Stand
❷ John Ireland Stand
❸ Billy Wright Stand
❹ Ring Road – St. Peters
❺ Waterloo Road
❻ A449 Stafford Street
❼ BR Station (½ mile)

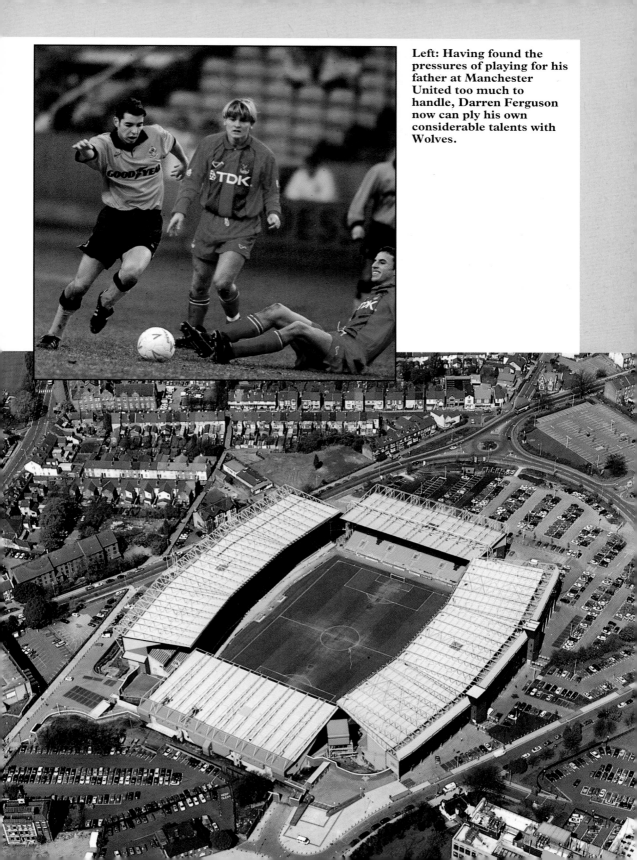

Left: Having found the pressures of playing for his father at Manchester United too much to handle, Darren Ferguson now can ply his own considerable talents with Wolves.

WREXHAM

Racecourse Ground, Mold Road, Wrexham, Clwyd LL11 2AN

Tel No: 0978 262129
Advance Tickets Tel No: 0978 262129
League: 2nd Division
Brief History: Founded 1873 (oldest Football Club in Wales). Former Ground: Acton Park, permanent move to Racecourse Ground c.1900. Founder-members Third Division North (1921). Record attendance 34,445.
(Total) Current Capacity: 17,500 (5,026 Seated)
Visiting Supporters' Allocation: 4,130 (2,230 Seated)

Club Colours: Red shirts, white shorts
Nearest Railway Station: Wrexham General
Parking (Car): (Nearby) Town car parks
Parking (Coach/Bus): As directed by Police
Police Force and Tel No: Wrexham Division (0978 290222)
Disabled Visitors' Facilities
  Wheelchairs: Mold Road Side
  Blind: Commentary available

KEY

C Club Offices
S Club Shop
E Entrance(s) for visiting supporters
R Refreshment bars for visiting supporters
T Toilets for visiting supporters

↑ North direction (approx)

❶ Wrexham General BR Station
❷ A541 – Mold Road
❸ Wrexham Town Centre
❹ Car Park
❺ Kop Town End

186

Right: Steve Watkin holds off the attentions of David Philips of Nottingham Forest in this Coca Cola Cup encounter in October 1993.

WYCOMBE WANDERERS

Adams Park, Hillbottom Road, Sands, High Wycombe, Bucks, HP12 4HU.

Tel No: 0494 472100
Advance Tickets Tel No: 0494 472100
League: 3rd Division
Brief History: Founded 1884. Former Grounds: The Rye, Spring Meadows, Loakes Park, moved to Adams Park 1990. Promoted to Football League 1993. Record attendance 15,678 (Loakes Park)
(Total) Current Capacity: 7,200 (1,267 Seated)
Visiting Supporters' Allocation: 500 (Seated 90 min.)

Club Colours: Cambridge and Oxford blue quartered shirts, blue shorts.
Nearest Railway Station: High Wycombe (2 1/2 miles)
Parking (Car): At Ground and Street parking
Parking (Coach/Bus): At Ground
Police Force and Tel No: Thames Valley 0296 396534
Disabled Visitors' Facilities
   Wheelchairs: Special shelter - Main Stand, Hillbottom Road end
   Blind: Commentary available

KEY

C Club Offices
S Club Shop
E Entrance(s) for visiting supporters
R Refreshment bars for visiting supporters
T Toilets for visiting supporters

↑ North direction (approx)

❶ Car Park
❷ Hillbottom Road (Industrial Estate)
❸ M40 Junction 4 (approx. 2 miles)
❹ Wycombe Town Centre (approx. 2 1/2 miles)

Left: Steve Guppy appeared in the 1993 F.A.Trophy Final, the last match the Wanderers played as a non-League team before their promotion to the Third Division.

YORK CITY

Bootham Crescent, York, YO3 7AQ

Tel No: 0904 624447
Advance Tickets Tel No: 0904 624447
League: 2nd Division
Brief History: Founded 1922. Former ground: Fulfordgate Ground, moved to Bootham Crescent in 1932. Record attendance 28,123.
(Total) Current Capacity: 12,475 (3,245 Seated)
Visiting Supporters Allocation: 3,980 (630 Seated)

Club Colours: Red shirts, blue shorts
Nearest Railway Station: York
Parking (Car): Street parking
Parking (Coach/Bus): As directed by Police
Police Force and Tel No: North Yorkshire (0904 631321)
Disabled Visitors' Facilities
    Wheelchairs: In front of Family Stand
    Blind: Commentary available

KEY

C Club Offices
S Club Shop
E Entrance(s) for visiting supporters
R Refreshment bars for visiting supporters
T Toilets for visiting supporters

↑ North direction (approx)

❶ Bootham Crescent
❷ Grosvenor Road
❸ Burton Stone Lane
❹ York BR Station (1 mile)

Right: John Jeffers of Port Vale takes on Gary Swann of York City during a top-of-the-table clash in April 1994.

HAMPDEN STADIUM

Hampden Park, Letherby Drive, Mount Florida, Glasgow, G42 9BA

Telephone: 041 632 1275

Brief History: Opened on 31 October, 1903 and used since as the Home Ground of Queen's Park F.C. (The oldest club in Scotland) used extensively for Scottish International matches - Record attendance: 150,239 (Scotland v England, April 1937).

(Total) Current Capacity: 35,000 all seated

Nearest Railway Station: Mount Florida or Kings Park

Parking (Car): Adjacent car park

Parking (Coach/Bus): Stadium car park.

Police Force and Tel No: Strathclyde 041 422 1113

Disabled Visitors Facilities
  Wheelchairs: Special Terrace
  Blind: Commentary available

Anticipated Development(s): Increase to 60,000 all Seated in 1996.

KEY

❶ Somerville Drive
❷ Cathcart Road
❸ Aikenhead Road
❹ Mount Florida BR Station
❺ Kings Park BR Station (1/2 mile)
❻ Parking
❼ Main Entrance

ABERDEEN

Pittodrie Stadium, Pittodrie Street, Aberdeen, AB2 1QH

Telephone: 0224 632328
League: Premier Division
Brief History: Founded 1881, amalgamated
with Orion and Victoria United in 1903,
Pittodrie Park used by the former Aberdeen
F.C. Record attendance: 45,061. Former
grounds: Links, Hayton, Holburn Cricket
Ground, Chanonry. Orion - Cattofield. Victoria
United - Central Park.
(Total) Current Capacity: 21,634 All Seated
Club Colours: Red Shirts, Red Shorts.

Nearest Railway Station: Aberdeen
Parking (Car): Beach Boulevard, King Street &
Golf Road
Parking (Coach/Bus): Beach Boulevard
Police Force and Tel No: Grampian 0224
639111
Disabled Visitors Facilities
Wheelchairs: Merkland Stand (prior
arrangement), Richard Donald Stand (season
pass)
Blind: No special facility.

KEY

C Club Offices
S Club Shop
E Entrance(s) for visiting
supporters
R Refreshment bars for visiting
supporters
T Toilets for visiting supporters

❶ Pittodrie Street
❷ Gold Road
❸ A92 King Street
❹ Aberdeen BR station (1 mile)
❺ Trinity Cemetery

Left: Eion Jess, an exciting discovery for Aberdeen and already rewarded with International honours, in action during September 1993.

CELTIC

Celtic Park, 95 Kerrydale Street, Glasgow, G40 3RE

Tel No: 041 556 2611
Advance Tickets Telephone: 041 551 8653
League: Premier Division
Brief History: Founded 1888. Former ground: (Old) Celtic Park until 1892. Founder members Scottish League (1890) Record attendance: 92,000.
(Total) Current Capacity: 49,856 (12,924 seated)
Visiting Supporters Allocation: 5,870 (50 seated)
Club Colours: Green & White Hooped Shirts, White Shorts

Nearest Railway Station: Bridgeton Cross
Parking (Car): Adjacent to ground.
Parking (Coach/Bus): Adjacent to ground.
Police Force and Tel No: Strathclyde 041 554 1113
Disabled Visitors Facilities
  Wheelchairs: North Enclosure (Permit Holders)
  Blind: Commentary available.
Anticipated Development(s): Major construction work to be undertaken (other events at Stadium eg Rock concerts not scheduled until completion)

KEY
C Club Offices
S Club Shop
E Entrance(s) for visiting supporters
R Refreshment bars for visiting supporters
T Toilets for visiting supporters

❶ A74 London Road
❷ A89 Gallowgate
❸ To Bridgeton Cross BR Station
❹ Springfield Road

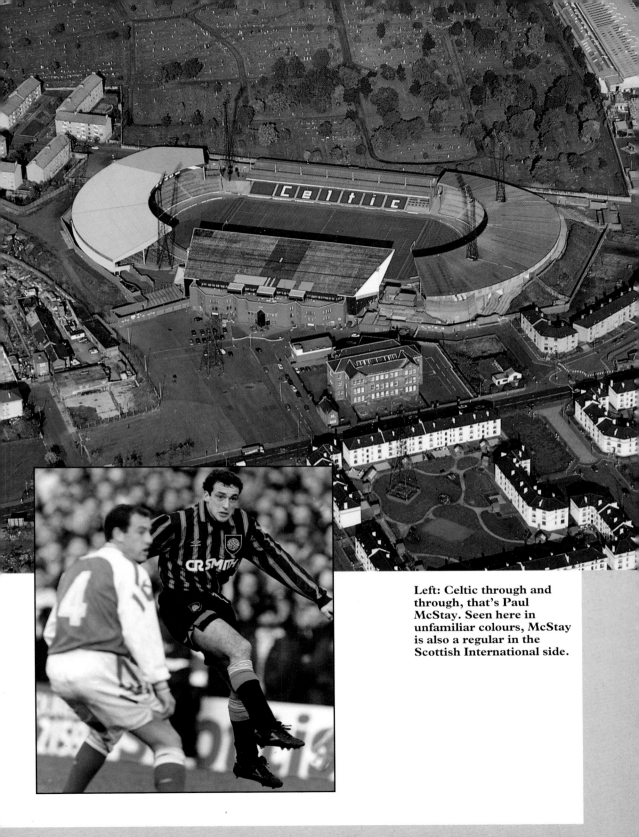

**Left: Celtic through and
through, that's Paul
McStay. Seen here in
unfamiliar colours, McStay
is also a regular in the
Scottish International side.**

DUNDEE UNITED

Tannadice Park, Tannadice Street, Dundee, DD3 7JW

Tel No: 0382 833166
League: Premier Division
Brief History: Founded 1909 as Dundee
Hibernian, changed name to Dundee United in
1923. Tannadice Park used previously by
former Scottish League members (1894/95)
Dundee Wanderers. Record attendance 28,000.
(Total) Current Capacity: 16,868 (7,680
seated)

Club Colours: Tangerine Shirts, Black Shorts
Nearest Railway Station: Dundee
Parking (Car): Street Parking & Gussie Park
Parking (Coach/Bus): Gussie Park
Police Force and Tel No: Tayside 0382 23200
Disabled Visitors Facilities
Wheelchairs: George Fox Stand & Tannadice
Street
Blind: Facility available

KEY

E Entrance(s) for visiting
supporters

❶ Dens Road
❷ Dundee F.C. Ground
❸ Sandemen Street
❹ Arklay Street
❺ Tannadice Street
❻ Dundee BR Station (1 mile)

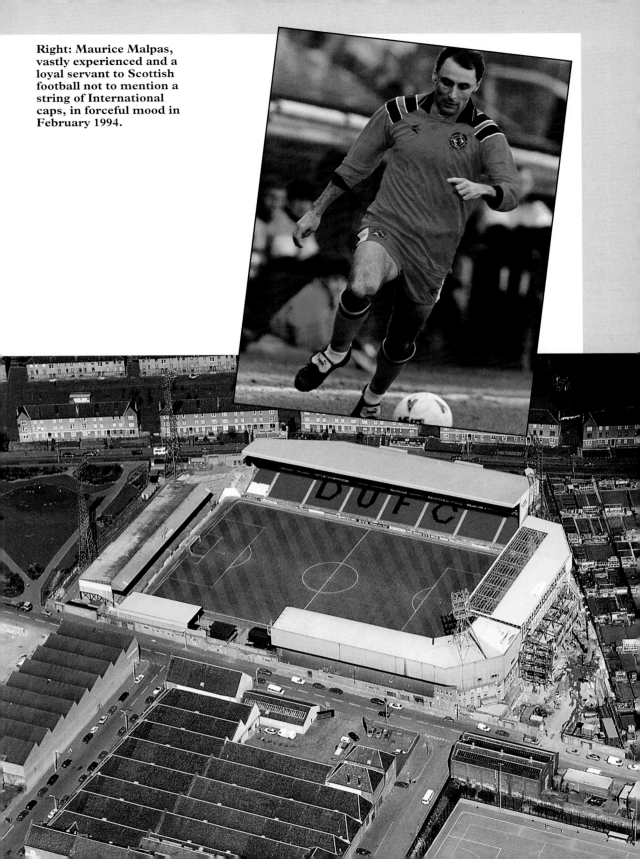

Right: Maurice Malpas, vastly experienced and a loyal servant to Scottish football not to mention a string of International caps, in forceful mood in February 1994.

HEART OF MIDLOTHIAN

Tynecastle Park, Georgie Road, Edinburgh, EH11 2NL

Tel No: 031 337 6132
Advance Tickets Telephone: 031 337 9011
League: Premier Division
Brief History: Founded 1874, founder members
Scottish League (1890). Former grounds: East
Meadows, moved to Powderhall in 1878,
Georgie Road (1881), Tynecastle (1886).
Record attendance: 53,496.
(Total) Current Capacity: 25,117 (10,000
seated)
Club Colours: Maroon Shirts, White Shorts.
Nearest Railway Station: Edinburgh
Haymarket

Parking (Car): Street Parking
Parking (Coach/Bus): Chesser Avenue
Police Force and Tel No: Lothian & Borders
031 229 2323
Disabled Visitors Facilities
Wheelchairs: 20 spaces total (8 for visiting
supporters)
Blind: Commentary available
Anticipated Development(s): Creation of three
new stands.

KEY
- **C** Club Offices
- **S** Club Shop
- **E** Entrance(s) for visiting supporters
- **R** Refreshment bars for visiting supporters
- **T** Toilets for visiting supporters

❶ Gorgie Road
❷ McLeod Street
❸ West Approach Road
❹ To Edinburgh Haymarket BR station

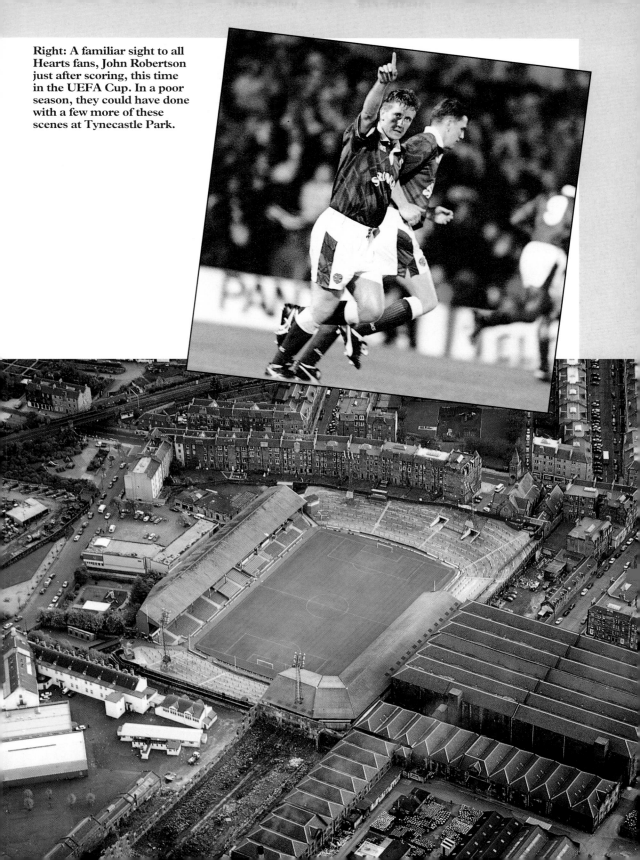

Right: A familiar sight to all Hearts fans, John Robertson just after scoring, this time in the UEFA Cup. In a poor season, they could have done with a few more of these scenes at Tynecastle Park.

RANGERS

Ibrox Stadium, 150 Edminston Drive, Glasgow, G51 3XD

Tel No: 041 427 8500
Advance Tickets Telephone: 041 427 8800
League: Premier Division
Brief History: Founded 1873. Founder Members Scottish League (1890). Former Grounds: Flesher's Haugh, moved to Burnbank (1875), Kinning Park (1876), Ibrox Park (1887) and Ibrox Stadium in 1899. Record attendance 118,567.
(Total) Current Capacity: 45,407 (38,407 seated)
Club Colours: Blue Shirts, White Shorts

Nearest Railway Station: Ibrox (underground)
Parking (Coach/Bus): Albion Training Ground
Police Force and Tel No: Strathclyde 041 445 1113
Disabled Visitors Facilities
  Wheelchairs: West enclosure
  Blind: West enclosure
Anticipated Development(s): Seating of enclosure to be completed by August 1994. Will make all seated stadium capacity 47,000.

KEY

C Club Offices
S Club Shop
E Entrance(s) for visiting supporters

❶ Edminston Drive
❷ Ibrox (Underground station)
❸ Copland Road
❹ Govan Stand
❺ M8 Motorway
❻ Broomloan Stand
❼ To Glasgow Central BR station

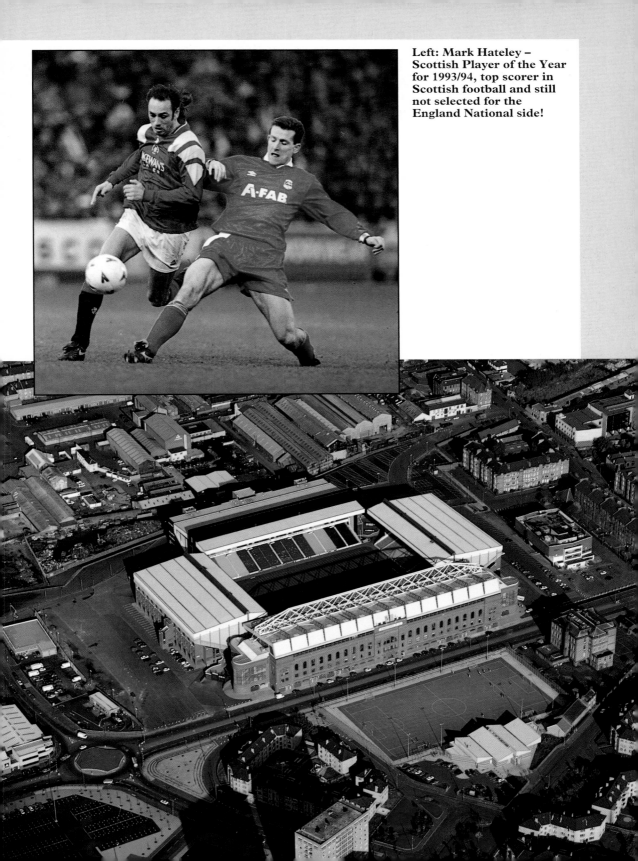

**Left: Mark Hateley –
Scottish Player of the Year
for 1993/94, top scorer in
Scottish football and still
not selected for the
England National side!**

AIRDRIEONIANS

**Broomfield Park,
Gartlea Road,
Airdrie, ML6 9JL**

League: Division 1
(Groundsharing with
Clyde F.C. 1994/95 season
until construction of new
ground)

ALBION ROVERS

**Cliftonhill Stadium,
Main Street,
Coatbridge,
Strathclyde,
ML5 3RB**

League: Division 3
(Will groundshare with
Aidrie eventually when new
Airdrieonians ground
completed)

ALLOA ATHLETIC

**Recreation Park,
Clackmannan Rd,
Alloa, FK10 1RR**

League: Division 3

ARBROATH

**Gayfield Park,
Arbroath,
DD11 1QB**

League: Division 3

AYR UNITED

**Somerset Park,
Tryfield Place,
Ayr, KA8 9NB**

League Division 1

BERWICK RANGERS

**Shielfield Park,
Shielfield Terrace,
Tweedmouth,
Berwick upon
Tweed, TD15 2EF**

League: Division 2

BRECHIN CITY

**Glebe Park,
Trinity Road,
Brechin, Angus,
DD9 6BJ**

League: Division 2

CALEDONIAN THISTLE

**Kingsmills Park,
Kingsmills Road,
Inverness**

League: Division 3
(Amalgamation of 'Inverness
Caledonian' and 'Inverness
Thistle' and elected to
Scottish League 1994/95
season)

CLYDE

**Broadwood
Stadium,
Cumbernauld,
Strathclyde**

League: Division 2

CLYDEBANK

**Kilbowie Park,
Arran Place,
Clydebank,
G81 2PB**

League: Division 1

COWDENBEATH

**Central Park,
High Street,
Cowdenbeath,
KY4 9EY**

League: Division 3

DUMBARTON

**Boghead Park,
Miller Street,
Dumbarton,
G82 2JA**

League: Division 2

DUNDEE

**Dens Park
Stadium,
Dens Road,
Dundee, DD3 7JY**

League: Division 1

DUNFERMLINE ATHLETIC

**East End Park,
Halbeath Road,
Dunfermline, Fife**

League: Division 1

EAST FIFE

**Bayview Park,
Wellesley Road,
Methil, Fifeshire,
KY8 3AG**

League: Division 2

EAST STIRLINGSHIRE

**Firs Park,
Firs Street,
Falkirk, FK2 7AY**

League: Division 3

FALKIRK

**Brockville Park,
Hope Street,
Falkirk, FK1 5AX**

League: Premier Division

FORFAR ATHLETIC

**Station Park,
Carseview Road,
Forfar, Tayside**

League: Division 3

GREENOCK MORTON

**Cappielow Park,
Sinclair Street,
Greenock,
PA15 2TY**

League: Division 2

HAMILTON ACADEMICAL

**Douglas Park,
Douglas Park Lane,
Hamilton,
ML3 0DF**

League: Division 1
(Expecting to groundshare
with Partick Thistle for
1994/95 season until
construction of new ground)

HIBERNIAN

**Easter Road
Stadium,
Albion Road,
Edinburgh,
EH7 5PG**

League: Premier Division

KILMARNOCK

**Rugby Park,
Rugby Road,
Kilmarnock,
Ayrshire, KA1 2DP**

League: Premier Division

MEADOWBANK THISTLE

Meadowbank Stadium, London Road, Edinburgh, EH7 65AE

League: Division 2 (Changing name to 'Livingston' in 1994)

MONTROSE

Links Park Stadium, Wellington Street, Montrose, DD10 8QD

League: Division 3

MOTHERWELL

**Fir Park,
Fir Park Street,
Motherwell,
ML1 2QN**

League: Premier Division

PARTICK THISTLE

**Firhill Park,
90, Firhill Road,
Glasgow, G20 7AL**

League: Premier Division

QUEEN OF THE SOUTH

Palmerston Park, Terregles Street, Dumfries

League: Division 2

QUEENS PARK

Hampden Park, Mount Florida, Glasgow, G42 9BA

League: Division 3
(NB * Play at Hampden Park, therefore covered in detail on pp 192-193)

RAITH ROVERS

**Stark's Park,
Pratt Street,
Kirkcaldy, KY1 1SA**

League: Division 1

ROSS COUNTY

**Victoria Park,
Dingwall,
Ross-shire,
IV15 9QW**

League: Division 3
(Elected to Scottish League
1994/95 season)

ST JOHNSTONE

**McDiarmid Park,
Crieff Road,
Perth, PH1 2SJ**

League: Division 1

ST MIRREN

**St Mirren Park,
Love Street,
Paisley, PA3 2EJ**

League: Division 1

STENHOUSEMUIR

**Ochilview Park,
Gladstone Road,
Stenhousemuir,
FK5 5QL**

League: Division 2

STIRLNG ALBION

**Forth Bank Stadium,
Spring Terse,
Stirling, FK7 7UJ**

League: Division 2

STRANRAER

**Stair Park,
London Road,
Stranraer,
DG9 8BS**

League: Division 1

Notes

Notes

Aerofilms Limited

Aerofilms was founded in 1919 and has specialised in the acquisition of aerial photography within the United Kingdom throughout its history. The company has a record of being innovative in the uses and applications of aerial photography.

Photographs looking at the environment in perspective are called oblique aerial photographs. These are taken with Hasselblad cameras by professional photographers experienced in the difficult conditions encountered in aerial work.

Photographs looking straight down at the landscape are termed vertical aerial photographs. These photographs are obtained using Leica survey cameras, the products from which are normally used in the making of maps.

Aerofilms has a unique library of oblique and vertical photographs in excess of one and a half million in number covering the United Kingdom. This library of photographs dates from 1919 to the present and is continually being updated.

Oblique and vertical photography can be taken to customers' specification by Aerofilms' professional photographers.

To discover more of the wealth of past or present photographs held in the library at Aerofilms or to commission new aerial photography to your requirements, please contact:

Aerofilms Limited
Gate Studios
Station Road
Borehamwood
Herts WD6 1EJ

Telephone 081-207-0666
Fax 081-207-5433

Readers who wish to purchase copies of any of the oblique aerial photographs featured in this book are referred to the order form which appears on another page.